Oxford Literacy Skills

Geoff Barton
Richard Broomhead
Fiona Edwards
Julie Macey

OXFORD

UNIVERSITY PRESS

OXFORD
UNIVERSITY PRESS

Great Clarendon Street, Oxford OX2 6DP

Oxford University Press is a department of the University of Oxford.
It furthers the University's objective of excellence in research, scholarship,
and education by publishing worldwide in

Oxford New York

Athens Auckland Bangkok Bogotá Buenos Aires Calcutta
Cape Town Chennai Dar es Salaam Delhi Florence Hong Kong Istanbul
Karachi Kuala Lumpur Madrid Melbourne Mexico City Mumbai
Nairobi Paris São Paulo Singapore Taipei Tokyo Toronto Warsaw

with associated companies in Berlin Ibadan

Oxford is a registered trade mark of Oxford University Press
in the UK and in certain other countries

ISBN 0 19 831466 3

Typeset by Pentacor plc, High Wycombe
Printed by Cambridge University Press

Contents

Introduction   5

Non-fiction and media

Unit 1   Giving the facts   6

Language focus   Presentational devices
                  Simple and complex sentences
       Text A   Information text: *Eyewitness Guides* – Future
       Text B   News website piece: *Bionic Man is on the Horizon*

Unit 2   Know your audience   21

Language focus   Informal writing
                  Noun phrase
       Text A   Advertising: Vauxhall Corsa brochure
       Text B   Newspaper article: *Royal Hatscot*

Unit 3   Setting the scene   32

Language focus   Adjectives
       Text A   Autobiography: *The Other Side of the Dale* by Gervase Phinn
       Text B   Promotional website page: *What to See in Nidderdale*

Drama

Unit 1   Introducing characters   43

Language focus   Dialogue
                  Stage directions
       Text A   Stage play: *St Joan* by George Bernard Shaw
       Text B   TV script: *The Vicar of Dibley* by Richard Curtis

Unit 2   The power of speech   68

Language focus   Features of informal speech
                  Australian slang and dialect

Text A   Stage play: *Two Weeks with the Queen* by Mary Morris
Text B   Poem: *Mid-term Break* by Seamus Heaney

Fiction

Unit 1   **And then...**   86

Language focus   Discourse markers
Text A   Story: *Black and White* by Rachel Anderson
Text B   Autobiography: *A Wilderness of Monkeys* by Gerald Durrell

Unit 2   **Looking at legends**   100

Language focus   Formal language
Text A   Legend: *Semer Water* by Mike Harding
Text B   Legend: *Theseus, Monster-Killer* by Tony Robinson and Richard Curtis

Unit 3   **Horror!**   112

Language focus   Using detail   Sentence length   Plot twists
Text A   Horror story: *The Dog Got Them* by Philippa Pearce
Text B   Poem: *The Trap* by Jon Stallworthy

Poetry

Unit 1   **Telling a tale**   125

Language focus   First person/third person
                Pronouns
                Rhyme (end, internal, full, sight, rhyming couplet)
                Text A Poem: *The Chimney Sweeper* by William Blake
                Text B Novel: *The Water Babies* by Charles Kingsley

Unit 2   **Finding a voice**   136

Language focus   Accent   Dialect
                Standard English   Black English
                Text A Poem: *Dis Poetry* by Benjamin Zephaniah
                Text B Poem: *Poetry* by John Hegley

                Glossary   147

Introduction to the teacher

Oxford Literacy Skills Book 1 is the first book of a three-book 'skills programme', which aims to improve your students' literacy skills between the ages of 11 and 14.

We have deliberately designed this book as a flexible resource. We know from our own experience as English teachers that the most useful classroom resources are the ones teachers – and students – can dip into easily. Although this book is divided into units, each unit contains freestanding activity packages – focusing on:

- grammar and language skills
- comprehension
- speaking and listening
- comparison of two contrasting texts
- extended writing.

If you wanted, and if time allowed, you could start at the beginning of each unit and work your way through – but at the same time it is possible to pick out just those skills you want to work on. (Each unit follows the same broad pattern of activities, to make selection easier.) For instance, you might guide your students through the grammar and language work, ask them to work individually on the comprehension activities, then form groups or pairs for a speaking and listening activity. Alternatively, you might want to concentrate on comprehension and extended writing assignments. You might have time to look at two texts, or you might instead prefer to focus on only one. The choice is yours.

All activities – with the obvious exception of Speaking and Listening tasks – have been phrased to allow for some sort of written outcome. However, you may prefer to use the language or comparison questions as class discussion activities, and then allow students to produce written answers for other activities. Certainly, many students coming up from Key Stage 2 will be used to 'shared', collaborative work on grammar and language, and you may want to extend this style of teaching into your language lessons in Key Stage 3. Our aim has been to leave as many options open to you and your students as possible.

We have also produced a series of Writing Frames – photocopiable sheets which will support your students as they work through these activities. You can download these, free of charge, from the website www.oup.co.uk/oxliteracyskills. Lastly, answers to all of the language, comprehension, and comparison questions appear in the photocopiable Answer Book which accompanies this Students' Book.

We have enjoyed putting this book together; we hope that you, and your students, enjoy using it.

Geoff Barton
Richard Broomhead
Fiona Edwards
Julie Macey

Non-fiction *and* media

Giving the facts

Aims

Aims

In this unit you will:

- learn about presentational devices in information texts
- look at how writers use different types of sentences for different purposes and audiences
- explore how knowing the meaning of prefixes can help you decode new or unfamiliar language
- compare an information text with a news feature from a website
- write persuasive and information texts – and create the villain for a new science fiction film.

Language focus

Before starting to write an information text, the writer has to decide

- how to lay out and present it
- what sort of language structures to use.

The right decisions will make an information text clear and easy to read. The wrong ones will make it jumbled and confusing.

Presentational devices

'Presentational devices' is the name for the various ways of laying out a text. These are also know as 'design features'. In an information text they can include:

- titles and headings
- subheadings
- captions and labels
- bullet points
- different font sizes
- bold lettering
- underlinings
- colour
- boxes and borders
- pictures/diagrams

Simple and complex sentences

These are two of the main sentence types. A writer will decide which to use depending on:

- what the purpose of the text is (to inform? persuade? instruct? entertain?)
- who the audience is.

Look at these examples:

Simple sentences

My name is C-3PO. I am a droid.
A droid is a mechanical being.

(from *I am a Droid by C-3PO* by Marc Cerasini)

This writing is in simple sentences. Each sentence has one main point so that the information is clear. Marc Cerasini has chosen to use simple sentences because he is writing for young children.

Complex sentences

But he seemed to me most glorious on Saturdays, when my mother took me to watch him play rugby at Rostyn Park. We sat in the old wooden stand, that could put splinters into the backs of your legs if you squirmed about too much.

(from *Gulf* by Robert Westall)

This writing is in complex sentences. A complex sentence contains more than one idea and can be made up of several clauses. One clause is the **main clause**, which deals with the main meaning of the sentence. There will also be one or more **subordinate clauses**, which give more information about what is happening, e.g.

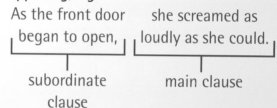

Remember that the subordinate clause is the part that adds more meaning to the sentence but would not make sense on its own.

Robert Westall has chosen complex sentences because

- he has more complex ideas to put across
- he is writing for an older audience, so he does not need to keep to simple sentences.

You are about to look at a piece of information writing which uses a lot of scientific and technical terms. Some of these may be unfamiliar to you. Knowing about prefixes could help you work out what these words mean.

Prefixes

Prefixes are elements that we add to the start of the base form of a word to change its meaning. For example:

un+happy   dis+obey
re+appear   super+hero

The more prefixes that you know, the easier you will find it to work out the meaning of new vocabulary as you come across it.

TEXT A

An information text for children (like the one on pages 10-11) has to grab the attention of the reader quickly. This text, published by Dorling Kindersley, has been set out for easy use by a child – though some of the language is actually quite technical. Dorling Kindersley is well known for its informational and factual texts – you probably have some in your school library.

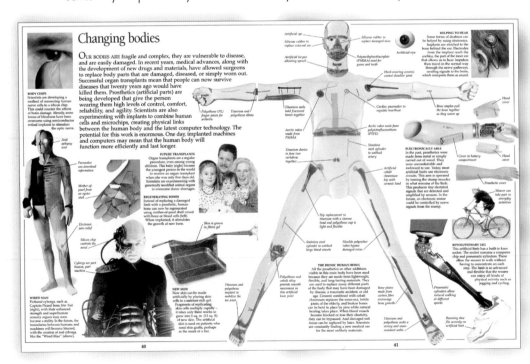

Language questions

1 In an information text you may need to find material quickly; the layout is meant to help you find what you need. See how quickly you can answer the next three questions (a, b and c):
a) How many pictures/illustrations can you see?
b) How many main paragraphs of text are there?
c) Where can you find out about a revolutionary leg?

2 Look back at the list of presentational devices on page 7. Which ones can you find examples of in the text? List the ones you find.

3 How would you describe the layout of this text overall?

▸ Clear?
▸ Cluttered?
▸ Easy to use?
▸ Too detailed?
▸ Other ideas of your own?

Explain your answer in a short paragraph. Give reasons why you came to your decision. (Your answers to question 1 will help you: how easy was it to find these answers?)

4 In the Language focus section you looked at two extracts from texts written for different audiences. Look at the paragraph 'Future Transplants'. This paragraph contains three simple sentences. Here is an example:

Organ transplants are a regular procedure, even among young children.

(Don't be caught out: a simple sentence might be quite long even though it is only about one idea!)
    Looking at the rest of the text, find an example of a simple sentence in each of these paragraphs:

▸ Body Chips
▸ New Skin
▸ Helping to Hear

Changing bodies

O**UR BODIES ARE** fragile and complex, they are vulnerable to disease, and are easily damaged. In recent years, medical advances, along with the development of new drugs and materials, have allowed surgeons to replace body parts that are damaged, diseased, or simply worn out. Successful organ transplants mean that people can now survive diseases that twenty years ago would have killed them. Prosthetics (artificial parts) are being developed that give the person wearing them high levels of control, comfort, reliability, and agility. Scientists are also experimenting with implants to combine human cells and microchips, creating physical links between the human body and the latest computer technology. The potential for this work is enormous. One day, implanted machines and computers may mean that the human body will function more efficiently and last longer.

BODY CHIPS
Scientists are developing a method of connecting human nerve cells to a silicon chip. This could counter the effects of brain damage. Already, some forms of blindness have been overcome using semiconductor retinal implants to stimulate the optic nerve.

Polyethene (PE) finger joints for arthritis

Titanium and polyethene elbow

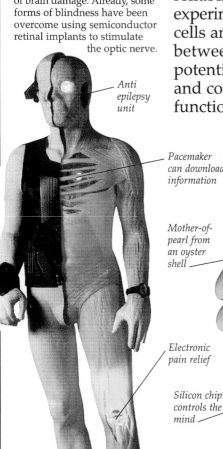

Anti epilepsy unit

Pacemaker can download information

Mother-of-pearl from an oyster shell

Electronic pain relief

Silicon chip controls the mind

Cyborgs are part human, part machine

WIRED MAN
Fictional cyborgs, such as Captain Picard from *Star Trek* (right), with their enhanced strength and superhuman sensory organs may soon become a reality. In the future, the boundaries between humans and machines will become blurred, with the creation of real cyborgs, like the "Wired Man" (above).

FUTURE TRANSPLANTS
Organ transplants are a regular procedure, even among young children. This baby (right) became the youngest person in the world to receive an organ transplant when she was only five days old. Scientists are experimenting with genetically modified animal organs to overcome donor shortages.

REGENERATING BONES
Instead of replacing a damaged limb with a prosthetic, human bone can now be regenerated using mother-of-pearl shell mixed with bone or blood cells (left). When implanted, it stimulates the growth of new bone.

Skin is grown in fibrin gel

NEW SKIN
New skin can be made artificially by placing skin cells in a nutrient-rich gel. Fragments of replicating skin cells multiply rapidly – it takes only three weeks to grow into 1 sq. m (11 sq. ft) of new skin. The artificial skin is used on patients who need skin grafts, perhaps as the result of a fire.

Titanium and polyethene implant to mobilize the toe joint

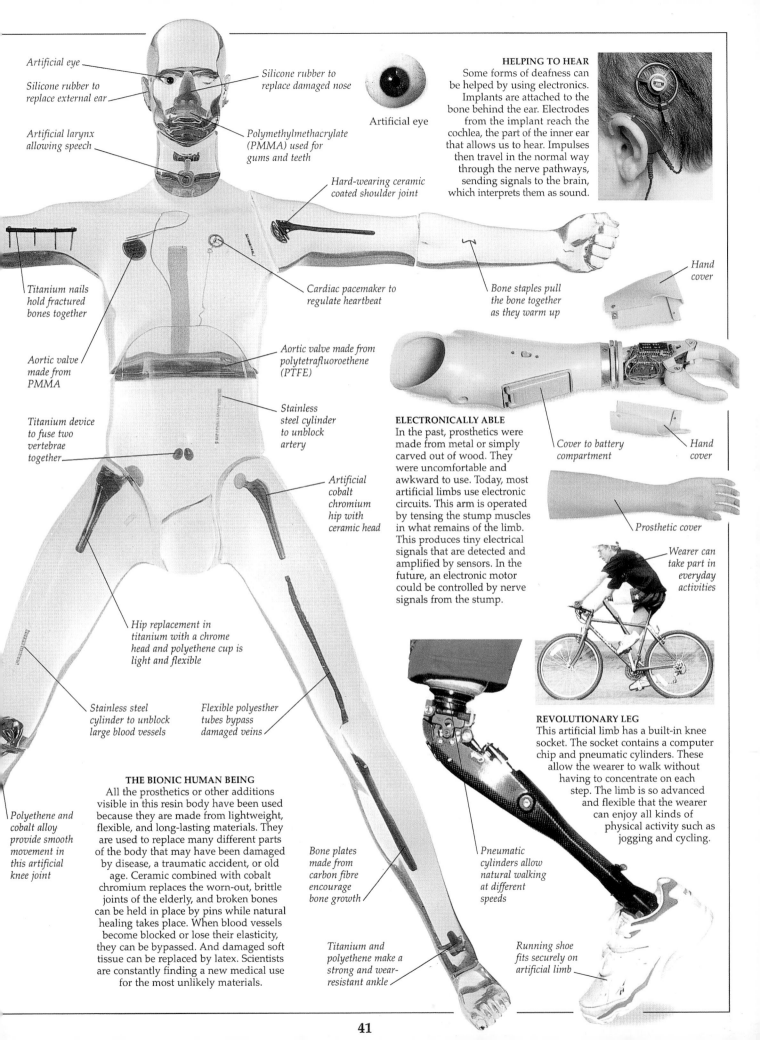

Artificial eye

Silicone rubber to replace external ear

Silicone rubber to replace damaged nose

Artificial larynx allowing speech

Artificial eye

Polymethylmethacrylate (PMMA) used for gums and teeth

Hard-wearing ceramic coated shoulder joint

HELPING TO HEAR
Some forms of deafness can be helped by using electronics. Implants are attached to the bone behind the ear. Electrodes from the implant reach the cochlea, the part of the inner ear that allows us to hear. Impulses then travel in the normal way through the nerve pathways, sending signals to the brain, which interprets them as sound.

Titanium nails hold fractured bones together

Cardiac pacemaker to regulate heartbeat

Bone staples pull the bone together as they warm up

Hand cover

Aortic valve made from PMMA

Aortic valve made from polytetrafluoroethene (PTFE)

Titanium device to fuse two vertebrae together

Stainless steel cylinder to unblock artery

ELECTRONICALLY ABLE
In the past, prosthetics were made from metal or simply carved out of wood. They were uncomfortable and awkward to use. Today, most artificial limbs use electronic circuits. This arm is operated by tensing the stump muscles in what remains of the limb. This produces tiny electrical signals that are detected and amplified by sensors. In the future, an electronic motor could be controlled by nerve signals from the stump.

Cover to battery compartment

Hand cover

Prosthetic cover

Artificial cobalt chromium hip with ceramic head

Wearer can take part in everyday activities

Hip replacement in titanium with a chrome head and polyethene cup is light and flexible

Stainless steel cylinder to unblock large blood vessels

Flexible polyesther tubes bypass damaged veins

Polyethene and cobalt alloy provide smooth movement in this artificial knee joint

REVOLUTIONARY LEG
This artificial limb has a built-in knee socket. The socket contains a computer chip and pneumatic cylinders. These allow the wearer to walk without having to concentrate on each step. The limb is so advanced and flexible that the wearer can enjoy all kinds of physical activity such as jogging and cycling.

THE BIONIC HUMAN BEING
All the prosthetics or other additions visible in this resin body have been used because they are made from lightweight, flexible, and long-lasting materials. They are used to replace many different parts of the body that may have been damaged by disease, a traumatic accident, or old age. Ceramic combined with cobalt chromium replaces the worn-out, brittle joints of the elderly, and broken bones can be held in place by pins while natural healing takes place. When blood vessels become blocked or lose their elasticity, they can be bypassed. And damaged soft tissue can be replaced by latex. Scientists are constantly finding a new medical use for the most unlikely materials.

Bone plates made from carbon fibre encourage bone growth

Pneumatic cylinders allow natural walking at different speeds

Titanium and polyethene make a strong and wear-resistant ankle

Running shoe fits securely on artificial limb

41

WORD BANK

agility ability to move quickly and easily

aortic to do with the main artery of the body (the aorta) which carries blood around the body

artery a blood-vessel inside the body

cardiac relating to the heart

cochlea part of the ear

efficiently (working) well with minimum waste or effort

larynx part of the throat which contains the vocal cords

replicating making a copy of itself

retinal to do with the retina, a part of the eye

silicon a non-metallic material

skin grafts transplanted skin

traumatic severe, very bad

5 Look at these examples of complex sentences:

> Although they have been around since ancient times, the greatest progress with artificial limbs has been made in the late twentieth century. Because technology has improved so quickly, it is now possible for people to live longer and lead healthier lives. Even though people will still get ill, it will be possible to fix major problems quickly and easily.

a) Rewrite these three complex sentences as six simple sentences.

b) How easy is it to understand the text now? Explain whether you think a young reader could follow your simple sentences more easily than the example above.

c) Why do you think most information texts for children are written in simple sentences? Write a sentence giving your opinion.

6 The text contains some scientific and technical words which may be difficult or new to a young reader. How might a reader work out what the unfamiliar words mean if they don't have a dictionary? If you understand the meaning of prefixes then you can hazard a guess at what a word might mean.

a) Look at the chart on the next page and complete it on your own.

Vocabulary	Prefix	Other words with this prefix	Possible meaning of prefix
transplants	trans	transport, translate, transcend	across – between two things
uncomfortable			
microchips			
superhuman			
regenerated			
interprets			
semiconductor			

b) Once you have completed this task, check in a dictionary to see how near you were to the definition.

7 Based on your study of the language of this extract, would you say that this text is:

▸ suitable for primary school children
▸ suitable for your age-group
▸ only suitable for older students who know a lot about the subject?

Write three or four sentences explaining why. Remember, you should base your answer on the language of the text (e.g. vocabulary, sentence types). Use examples from the text to back up your opinion.

Comprehension

1 Give three reasons why a surgeon might replace body parts.
Hint Look in the introduction.

2 What could a person gain from having artificial parts? Find three points in the text.

3 What do you think are the four most important words in the paragraph 'Helping to Hear'? List them.

4 Many people need organ transplants, but not enough people are willing to have their organs used after their death. What are scientists doing to solve this problem? Write a sentence to explain.
Hint Look in the paragraph 'Future Transplants'.

5 Read the paragraph 'New Skin'. Pick out the word that means 'not natural'.

6 a) If you wanted to find out about making bones, which heading would you look under?
b) Write a sentence to describe the process of making bones.

7 Captain Picard, a character from *Star Trek*, is featured in this text. Can you suggest a reason why the writer might have included this character?

8 Labels have been included alongside pictures. Why? Choose the most suitable answer:

▶ to explain what the picture is about
▷ to introduce the text
▶ to fill the space
▷ the writer got bored of using paragraphs.

9 Does the writer think that medical advances are improving the quality of a person's life? Base your answer (in a short paragraph) on the paragraph 'Electronically Able'. Give at least two reasons to back up your answer.

Speaking and listening

1 **Class**

Your class has been asked to take part in trials for a new brain implant. If it works, it will give you the power of telepathy (ability to communicate mind-to-mind, without any speech). Nobody knows yet whether it will work or what the side effects may be.

Divide into two groups. One group is going to compile arguments for this trial and one group will devise arguments against. Do not show each other your arguments. You will then hold a class debate on whether to go ahead with the trials or not. Your teacher will lead the debate.

Everyone should aim to say something in the debate , so you each need to write at least one argument.

At the end of the session your teacher will ask the class to vote on whether you should take part in the trials or not.

(Keep your notes for Writing Assignment 2.)

2 **Small groups**

Your group has been asked to create a cyborg character for a new science fiction film. (A cyborg is part-human, part-machine.) You have been sent the brief below and have to work to the writer's description:

Set on fictional planet of Atar in 22nd century — character can be male or female — has superhuman strength and intelligence — character will be a 'baddie' in the film and feared by other characters.

Make notes on your character. You need to include:

- your character's name
- what special features it has
- what sort of crimes it will commit.

You could plan your cyborg by drawing an outline of a body and adding labels to show which parts are mechanical.

(Keep your notes for Writing Assignment 3.)

WORD BANK

capability having the power to do something

human physiology how the body works

neural prosthetics parts that are connected to the brain

neurons nerve cells

to surpass to be better or greater than

TEXT B

The following report came from the ABC News website. *The Six Million Dollar Man* was a popular television programme in the 1970s. The main character, Steve Austin, was an astronaut severely injured in an accident. Surgeons rebuilt his body, giving him an artificial arm, eye, and legs: he could run faster than any other human being, lift heavy weights, and see through solid objects. This report is about how near technology has come to turning science fiction into scientific fact.

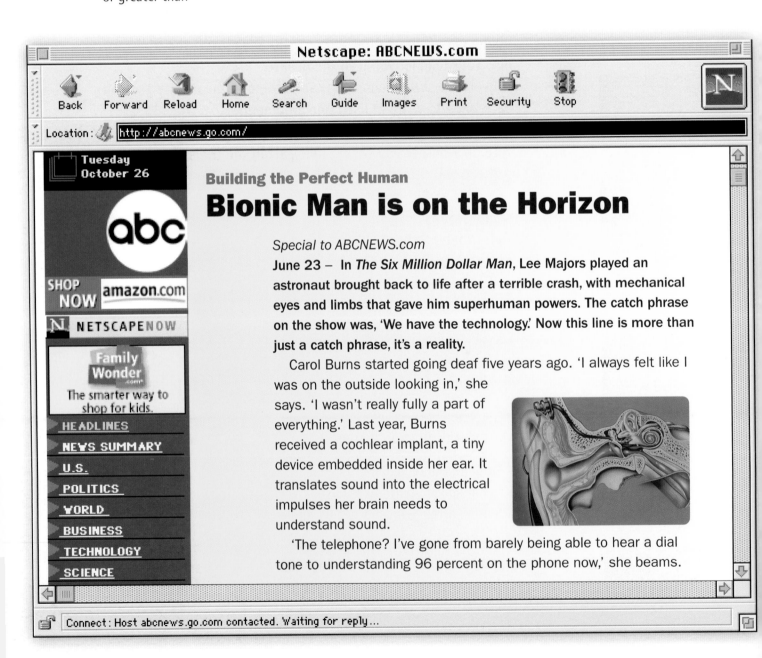

Netscape: ABCNEWS.com

Back | Forward | Reload | Home | Search | Guide | Images | Print | Security | Stop

Location: http://abcnews.go.com/

Tuesday October 26

Building the Perfect Human

Bionic Man is on the Horizon

Special to ABCNEWS.com

June 23 – In *The Six Million Dollar Man*, Lee Majors played an astronaut brought back to life after a terrible crash, with mechanical eyes and limbs that gave him superhuman powers. The catch phrase on the show was, 'We have the technology.' Now this line is more than just a catch phrase, it's a reality.

Carol Burns started going deaf five years ago. 'I always felt like I was on the outside looking in,' she says. 'I wasn't really fully a part of everything.' Last year, Burns received a cochlear implant, a tiny device embedded inside her ear. It translates sound into the electrical impulses her brain needs to understand sound.

'The telephone? I've gone from barely being able to hear a dial tone to understanding 96 percent on the phone now,' she beams.

SHOP NOW amazon.com

NETSCAPENOW

Family Wonder
The smarter way to shop for kids.

HEADLINES
NEWS SUMMARY
U.S.
POLITICS
WORLD
BUSINESS
TECHNOLOGY
SCIENCE

Connect: Host abcnews.go.com contacted. Waiting for reply...

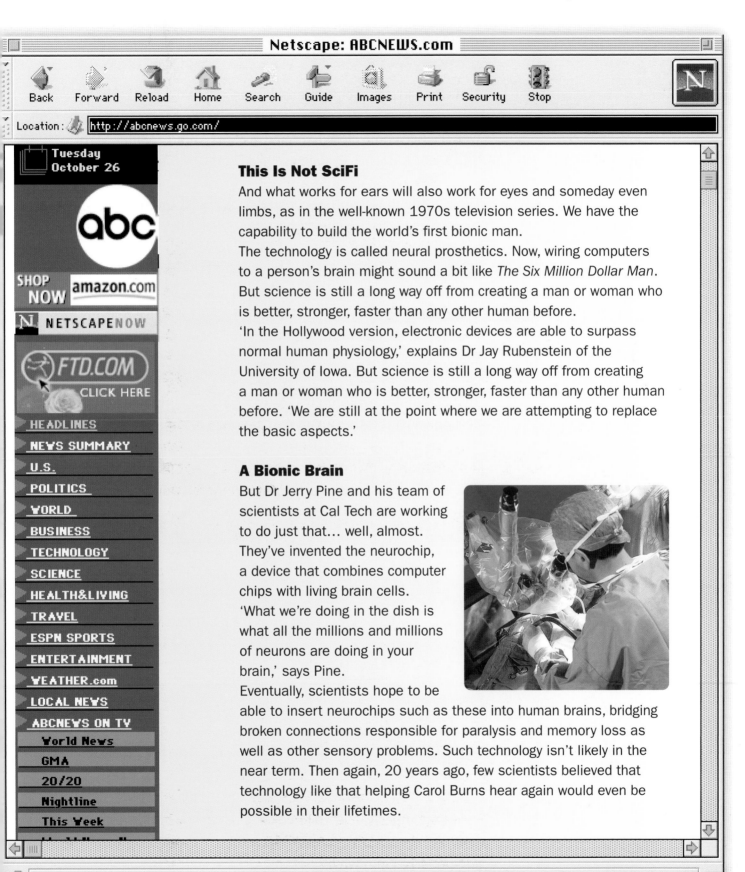

Netscape: ABCNEWS.com

Tuesday
October 26

This Is Not SciFi

And what works for ears will also work for eyes and someday even limbs, as in the well-known 1970s television series. We have the capability to build the world's first bionic man.

The technology is called neural prosthetics. Now, wiring computers to a person's brain might sound a bit like *The Six Million Dollar Man*. But science is still a long way off from creating a man or woman who is better, stronger, faster than any other human before.

'In the Hollywood version, electronic devices are able to surpass normal human physiology,' explains Dr Jay Rubenstein of the University of Iowa. But science is still a long way off from creating a man or woman who is better, stronger, faster than any other human before. 'We are still at the point where we are attempting to replace the basic aspects.'

A Bionic Brain

But Dr Jerry Pine and his team of scientists at Cal Tech are working to do just that... well, almost. They've invented the neurochip, a device that combines computer chips with living brain cells.

'What we're doing in the dish is what all the millions and millions of neurons are doing in your brain,' says Pine.

Eventually, scientists hope to be able to insert neurochips such as these into human brains, bridging broken connections responsible for paralysis and memory loss as well as other sensory problems. Such technology isn't likely in the near term. Then again, 20 years ago, few scientists believed that technology like that helping Carol Burns hear again would even be possible in their lifetimes.

Comparison

1 How has surgery helped Carol Burns?

2 Has science come close to creating a 'Six Million Dollar Man'?
Hint Look at what Dr Rubenstein says about this.

3 What is the name of the special device which might be able to help people who are paralysed?

4 What presentational devices do you notice in this text?

5 Who would you say this text is aimed at? Try to give reasons for your ideas, based on the language and vocabulary used in the report.

6 Text A is an information text: it was written to inform and describe. What is the purpose of Text B?

7 Both texts provide information to the reader but are very different in how they have been written. Compare the texts by copying and completing the checklist below.

	Text A	Text B
Which one is		
most informative?		
most detailed?		
more personal?		
most factual?		
presented the best?		
easiest to understand?		
most interesting?		

Write a comparison of the two texts using your information from the chart. At the end, add a sentence explaining which text you preferred and why.

Writing assignments

1 A futuristic company has asked you to produce a leaflet encouraging people to have worn-out body parts replaced. In your writing you will need to:

- set your leaflet out in an interesting way like Text A (use pictures/diagrams/headings)
- explain how replacing parts could improve someone's life (look back at Carol Burns in Text B)
- try to persuade the readers with positive language e.g. 'You too could feel like new'
- avoid overloading the reader with too much information – it could put them off.

2 One day brain implants may be available to all of us. Imagine you have been asked to produce a government health information sheet:

Brain implants – good or bad?

The text has to cover the arguments for and against this idea. (If you took part in Speaking and Listening activity 1, your notes from this will help you.)
In your writing try to:

- introduce the topic simply so that it is clear what it is about
- point out the advantages and disadvantages of implants
- give facts about implants
- think about how to present information (look back at the presentational devices in Text A)
- decide on a lively and catchy title or headline.

3 You are in charge of promoting a new science fiction video game, featuring the villain from Speaking and Listening activity 2. You have been asked to design a promotional advertisement to appear in a magazine.
You will need to:

- decide on your target audience (who the game is aimed at)

- use language that your audience will know (e.g. you might decide to use the latest slang if your advertisement is aimed at a young audience
- think about how to present the advert to attract people's attention (look back at presentational devices)
- inform the reader of what the game involves, where to buy it and what it is called (make it sound exciting and interesting)
- explain about your villain and how he or she features in the game (use the information from Speaking and Listening activity 2).

Remember that the purpose of the advertisement is to inform and persuade.

Non-fiction and media

Know your audience

Aims

In this unit you will:
- study how informal language can be used to appeal to an audience
- learn about how noun phrases can add detail to writing
- compare advertising 'copy' with a tabloid newspaper article
- learn about puns and how they are used in writing
- use informal language, slang and puns in your own writing.

Language focus

Writers of advertisements have to use language to attract particular audiences. The language of advertising tends to feature short, snappy sentences and adopt a chatty, friendly tone (much like a tabloid newspaper). Advertising often uses an informal but informative style to attract the reader's interest as quickly as possible.

Informal writing
This sort of writing can break the rules of grammar by using slang, changing sentence structure and sometimes appearing more like spoken language than written. Tabloid newspaper headlines and advertisements tend to use informal language.

Writers of advertisements and newspaper articles need to fit as much information as possible into a few words. To help them do so, they use noun phrases.

Noun phrase

A noun phrase is a group of words built around a naming word, or noun. Noun phrases allow the writer to add detail to their nouns and they are also good indicators of how detailed a text is.

For example:

the bus

the red bus

the old red bus

the old red rusty bus

WORD BANK

alloy a type of metal
exhilaration great excitement
spoiler a device on a car to improve road performance at speed

TEXT A

This extract is from a promotional leaflet for a Vauxhall Corsa car. It is aimed at young drivers.

Love life
Love SXi

If you love life, you'll love living with the Corsa SXi. This very special edition takes Corsa's lively personality into the next generation. The SXi is here – it's grown up, and it's sexy.

This sporty little model strikes a pose with alloy wheels, tinted glass and a smart rear spoiler. And with four cool colours to choose from this hot three-door hatch is sure to suit your style. But there's more to the SXi than scorching good looks. Inside you'll find sports front seats, a leather-covered steering wheel and a serious six speaker stereo.

The nippy 1.2i 16-valve SXi comes with a close-ratio gearbox and Lotus-tuned sports suspension for maximum exhilaration. Add power-assisted steering and your parking problems are over.

Of course, all the usual safety and security features you'd expect of a Vauxhall are there but at a price that may just surprise you.

Love life? You'll love Corsa SXi.

Language questions

1 The following words are used informally in the text:

> sexy
> smart
> cool
> hot
> scorching good looks
> serious six speaker stereo
> nippy

For each word or phrase, try to think of a more formal word or phrase which could be used.

2 How would you describe the overall tone of the writing?

- ▶ relaxed?
- ▶ light-hearted?
- ▶ serious?

Write a sentence explaining your ideas.

3 Explain why you think the writer has chosen to use informal language.

4 If the audience of the text were to be changed to, say, car buyers in their fifties, it is most likely that the style would be more formal. Try reworking a sentence of the advert for an older age group. For example:

> And with four <u>cool</u> colours to choose from this <u>hot</u> three-door hatch is sure to <u>suit your style</u>.

might be changed to

> And with four <u>special</u> colours to choose from this <u>desirable</u> three-door hatch is sure to <u>meet your needs</u>.

Read your new version to a few people in your class to see what they think.

Write an explanation of how well your new version went.

5 The writer uses noun phrases to add detail and tempt the reader. For example:

> very special edition

– edition is the noun here, the other words add more detail.

a) Find four more examples of noun phrases in Text A.

b) Try to write a short paragraph saying why you think the writer uses noun phrases quite often in this text. Think about:

▶ how building up detail might tempt the reader

▶ how it gives a clearer picture of the car and its features.

Try to give examples from the text to support your points.

Comprehension

1 What does 'Special Edition' suggest about the car? Write a sentence to explain.

2 Pick out a word or phrase in the first paragraph that shows that the leaflet is aimed at young drivers.

3 The reader is addressed as 'you'. Why is this? Pick the best answer from this list:

▶ The writer has no idea who will read the booklet.

▶ So that you feel as though it is written for you.

▶ The writer wants to be polite.

4 Find two examples in the first paragraph where the car is made to seem human. (This is known as personification.)

5 The brochure says that this car is 'sure to suit your style'. Find one feature listed in the brochure which supports this statement.

6 Find the word in the third paragraph which suggests that the car is fast.

7 The important point (the price) is not given but we are told that it 'may just surprise you'. What does this suggest?

8 How would you describe the text?

- persuasive
- over the top
- short, snappy and direct
- typical sales language

Write a paragraph to explain your answer.

Speaking and listening

1 **Group/class**

The writer of the text uses personification to make the Corsa seem like a person. What sort of person do you think the Corsa is, based on the text?

Make notes on your own first and then join into a group of three or four. As a group, listen to and discuss each other's ideas and then devise a whole group character profile using the guide below.

Name:
Age:
Job:
Hobbies/interests:
Where he/she lives (place and type of building):
Favourite colour:
Favourite food:
Preferred holiday resort:
Favourite type of music:
Favourite film:

Compare each group's ideas as a whole class. This could be a group presentation where each of you has to say something to the rest of the class.

Finally, as a class, discuss the following questions:

▷ Why did Vauxhall choose this personality?
▷ What other sorts of personality might have worked?

2 Group

In a group of three, you are going to improvise a scene at a car showroom. You should each play one of these parts:

▷ customer
▷ sales assistant
▷ observer.

Decide which role you are each going to take, then read the information below for your character.

Customer

On your own, write a profile of your character. Note down what sort of person you are. (Remember, you are creating a character, so you can adopt any personality you like.) What features are you looking for in a car? Speed? Safety? Something which will impress people? Do you want an expensive car but can't afford one? Or do you think cars are overpriced and just useful for getting about in?

Keep your profile to yourself before the role play begins: it is the sales assistant's job to find out what you are like and what your needs are, and then try to sell you a car based on what you want.

Sales assistant

Your role is to sell a car to the customer, but before you can do that, you will have to work out what he/she is like and what he/she wants from the car. Once you have worked this out, you need to pick phrases which will persuade him/her to buy the car. For instance, if the customer seems to be a show-off, you might like to impress them with a lot of technical car language and a list of all the things that the car can do; whereas if they are worried about expense, words like 'economical' and 'cheap to run' will appeal to them.
Note down:
▷ some questions for the customer, to help you find out what they want
▷ some persuasive words and interesting noun phrases which you can use to describe the car to them.

Observer
Your job is to observe the role play and make notes on what happens and what is said. Whilst the other two are planning you could create a list of what you are going to look for e.g. the use of noun phrases, persuasive words, a polite and friendly manner.

When you are all ready, run through the role play. The observer will take notes. Remember that you cannot rehearse: this is an improvisation, so you will have only one chance.

Once you have finished, come out of role but stay as a group of three. Talk about how well you think it went. You could consider these questions:

▶ Which persuasive words/language were most successful?
▶ Did the sales assistant use any noun phrases to add more detail?
▶ Was the atmosphere appropriate or did one character feel awkward?
▶ Could the characters have reacted differently?
▶ What could have been improved?

TEXT B

The text on the next page is a news report from *The Sun* newspaper, which is a tabloid. Royal Ascot is a horse-racing event held in June each year. On one particular day, known as 'Ladies' Day', female racegoers compete with each other to see who can wear the most extravagant hat...

WORD BANK

punters people who gamble or place bets
titfer Cockney rhyming slang for hat ('tit for tat')
toffs upper-class people

Look who's a-head in this year's fashion stakes

ROYAL HATSCOT

High society... a woman wears towering cone of flowers

AND they're on! Lady racegoers turned Ascot into Royal Hatscot yesterday as they shaded themselves from the blazing sun with amazing headgear.

There were some incredible odds – including one woman who plaiced her bets in a titfer covered in fish and chips.

Another fashion favourite wore a towering cone covered in flowers with a circle of blooms in front of her face. And one race fan beat the heat with a transparent number made from a swirl of feathers.

Among the toffs jockeying for position in the Royal Enclosure was tycoon's ex Ivana Trump, 49 – but she managed to make do with a modest cream hat with some simple decoration.

Classy chick... race fan in feathered number

Even the Queen won cheers for her wide-brimmed lilac number as she arrived in an open-top carriage.

Prince Philip and Prince Charles were with her, but Charles clutched an umbrella despite the heat. A relaxed Queen Mum was also in the procession.

Later Charles tried to drive off in his green Aston Martin but stalled as he revved his engine in front of crowds. He was cheered as he finally pulled away.

Almost £2.5 million in prize money is at stake for owners, trainers and jockeys this week.

Punters will eat and drink their way through 110,000 bottles of champagne, 2.2 tonnes of smoked salmon, four tonnes of strawberries and 520 gallons of cream.

Hattagirl... smiling Ivana

Cods-on favourite... fish'n chips

Comparison

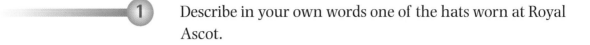

1 Describe in your own words one of the hats worn at Royal Ascot.

2 Why was Charles cheered by crowds?

3 What food is on the menu at the race meeting?

4 The style of Text A was informal. The style of this text is also informal, mainly due to the use of puns. A pun is when a word or phrase can have more than one meaning; the words are played upon. As in the first text, the tone here is friendly and chatty.

a) Below are several examples of puns from the report. Try to explain in your own words what you think the pun means. (The puns are underlined for you.)

> Look who's <u>a-head</u> in this year's fashion stakes
> Royal <u>Hatscot</u>
> And <u>they're on</u>
> There were some incredible <u>odds</u> – including one woman who <u>plaiced</u> her bets in a titfer covered in fish and chips

b) Find two more puns yourself and explain them.

5 In Text A you looked at the use of noun phrases. These are also found in tabloid newspapers: this type of writing lends itself to the use of sensational and lively noun phrases.

Copy the chart on the following page. For each example decide whether or not it is a noun phrase (Yes/No), and then change it into another colourful noun phrase to suit this style of writing.

Example	Noun phrase?	Own version
blazing sun	Yes	scorching rays
amazing headgear		
fashion favourite		
engine		
transparent number		
modest cream hat		
wide-brimmed lilac number		
umbrella		
tycoon's ex Ivana Trump, 49		

Writing assignments

1 Write a tabloid newspaper report based on this title:

Tycoon's ex Ivana turns heads in sporty new Corsa

In your writing you will need to:
- write an opening topic sentence (in bold) which summarizes the entire story
- keep sentences short, clear and lively
- use colourful noun phrases to add detail and create an informal style
- use puns to add humour.

You could refer back to the Corsa advertisement for ideas on how Ivana turned heads in the new car.

2 Royal Ascot decide that they need to attract younger racegoers to Ladies' Day. Write the brochure that they produce to persuade people to go.

You will need to:

- keep the writing informal, lively and short
- use noun phrases and persuasive words to attract younger people (as in the Corsa advert)
- explain what there is to do and see at Royal Ascot (use the report for information).

(For ideas for presentational devices to use when planning your leaflet, look back at the list in Unit 1, on page 7.)

3 Rewrite the Corsa advert changing the 'personality' of the car. You will need to decide on a personality first – for instance, someone who is a show-off.

You will need to:

- brainstorm ideas based on your chosen personality
- write about the car as though it is human (look back at how it is done in the advert)
- try to keep the writing lively, short and snappy so that the reader stays interested
- use words and phrases that will persuade the reader
- use noun phrases to build up description.

Non-fiction *and* media
Setting the scene

Aims

In this unit you will:

- study how adjectives can be used to give life to writing and to create particular effects
- understand how language can help the reader to picture the scene
- look at the use of fact and opinion in writing
- compare a piece of autobiographical writing with a tourist website – both about the same part of England
- use adjectives in your own writing to gain effects.

Language focus

Adjectives
An adjective is a describing word that adds meaning to a noun. For example:

the red car ('red' tells us more about the car)

a huge green caterpillar ('huge' describes how big the creature is but 'green' also describes its colour)

TEXT A

Gervase Phinn was a teacher for several years and then became an Inspector of English and Drama in North Yorkshire. His autobiography recounts his experiences in the Yorkshire countryside, visiting schools. In this extract he is searching for a small village school.

🍂 *The other side of the dale* 🍂

At long last, after a two-hour search up and down the Dale, along <u>muddy</u> twisting roads, across narrow <u>stone</u> bridges, up dirt tracks, past swirling rivers and <u>dribbling</u> streams, and through <u>countless</u> villages in an increasingly desperate search, I had eventually arrived at my destination. At the sight of the highly-polished brass plate on the door bearing the word BACKWATERSTHWAITE SCHOOL, I heaved a great sigh of relief and felt that sort of pioneering triumph which Christopher Columbus, Captain Cook and Scott of the Antarctic must have felt on arriving at their destinations after their difficult journeys.

I had seen no school sign, no traffic triangle warning of a school and children crossing, no playground, playing field,

WORD BANK

austere stern
beck a stream
creviced grew in narrow gaps
edifice a building
elusive difficult to find
gaunt grim, desolate
lichen a type of fungus
sturdy robust, strongly built
vain without success

nothing that would identify the austere building as an educational institution. The tall, gaunt edifice deep in the dark valley looked like any other large, sturdy Yorkshire country house and I had passed it unknowingly several times during my vain attempt to discover the elusive school. Beneath the slate roof, greasy grey and edged with a pale purple lichen, tall leaded windows faced the ever-watchful fields. From the grey and white limestone walls gillyflowers and tiny ferns creviced. A little beck trickled alongside as I made my way to the heavy oak door. At long last I had arrived. I lifted the great grey iron knocker in the shape of a ram's head and let it fall with a heavy echoing thud.

I had arrived at Upperwatersthwaite much earlier in the afternoon assuming, quite foolishly, that it was somewhere near Backwatersthwaite. As soon as I stepped through the door of the small village post office to ask for directions, all conversation ceased and every eye was directed my way. There were two sturdy, middle-aged women in thick brown woollen headscarves which were tied in enormous knots under their chins, a lean old farmer, clutching his pension book, who plucked the ancient pipe from his mouth at the sight of the stranger, and a young woman who jerked her toddler close to her when I made my entrance. I must have looked singularly out of place in the dark grey suit, formal college tie and white shirt. My black briefcase, with an official looking crest emblazoned on the front, was eyed suspiciously by the large, healthy-looking postmistress. She looked over the counter with a deadpan expression on her round red face. I joined what I took to be the end of the queue but was ushered forward by the pensioner.

Gervase Phinn

Language questions

1 Look at the opening paragraph. Several adjectives have been underlined for you. See if you can find eight more. Write them out in a list.

(Remember to ask yourself if your words describe something.)

2 This is the opening section without adjectives:

> At last, after a search up and down the Dale, along roads, across bridges, up tracks, past rivers and streams and through villages in a search, I had eventually arrived at my destination.

How different is the extract? Is it easy to picture the scene? Write a short explanation of your ideas.

3 Rewrite this passage, removing the adjectives:

> Beneath the slate roof, greasy grey and edged with a pale purple lichen, tall leaded windows faced the ever-watchful fields. From the grey and white limestone walls gillyflowers and tiny ferns creviced. A little beck trickled alongside as I made my way to the heavy oak door.

How does your new version change your understanding of the scene? Write a sentence explaining your answer.

Comprehension

1 How long has Gervase Phinn been searching for the school?

2 Find three words or phrases, which show that the scene is set in the countryside.

3 He compares his arrival with that of three famous explorers. Who are they?

4 How does the writer feel when he eventually finds the school? Explain in a sentence.

5 The school is described as being unpleasant looking. Pick a word in paragraph two to show this.

6 List who exactly is in the Post Office when Gervase Phinn enters (give as much information as you can).

7 How does Gervase Phinn feel when the people in the Post Office look at him? Choose the best answer:

▶ happy
▶ welcomed
▶ out of place

8 The postmistress looks 'over the counter with a deadpan expression'. What does this mean? Choose the most suitable answer:

▶ she is pleased to see him
▶ she is confused as she does not know what he wants
▶ she is really tired
▶ she looks serious without any expression on her face

9 Do you think that the people in the Post Office are used to seeing visitors like Gervase Phinn? Explain your answer in a short paragraph.

Speaking and listening

1 **Groups**
Imagine that the occupants of the Post Office discuss Gervase Phinn after he has left. What do you think each one would say? Do they all believe his explanation that he is looking for Backwatersthwaite School, or do they think he has come with

a different – perhaps sinister – purpose? Could he be a government official sent to check out the Post Office, an estate agent looking to buy property, a solicitor with news of a will? Do they all feel threatened by him, or do some of them think he might bring good news?

You will need to take parts as the following characters:

- the two middle-aged women
- the lean old farmer
- a young woman with a toddler (the child need not be a character)
- the postmistress.

Before you start, decide what your character's view of Gervase Phinn will be.

You might want to use this example as the opening of your role play:

Postmistress	He had me worried for a moment; it's not often that we get strangers in here.
Middle-aged woman	Yes, he didn't look the sort that we normally see in here.

2 Groups

Some people think that Gervase Phinn uses too many adjectives in this extract and that it spoils the scene. What do you think? In small groups discuss this idea and come up with an answer that you all agree on.

Ask yourselves these questions:
- Why has he used adjectives?
- Does he present the scene clearly?
- Does his use of double adjectives such as 'muddy twisting', 'narrow stone' and 'tall leaded' add anything extra to the description?

TEXT B

This passage is from an internet website about Nidderdale, a region in the Yorkshire Dales. Adjectives are again used to describe the place but in a more persuasive way so that the reader might be tempted to visit the area.

What to see in Nidderdale

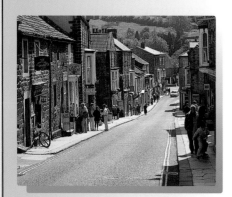

The attractive market town of Pateley Bridge, with its colourful floral displays and friendly people, is the self-styled capital of Nidderdale. Set against a steep hillside, the town offers a wide variety of speciality shops, cosy tearooms and welcoming public houses.

Explore a little further and you will discover its hidden treasures.

Visit the award-winning Nidderdale Museum, the Pateley Playhouse 'Little Theatre of the Dales' and the creative talents of a potter, jeweller and glassblower hard at work in their craft workshops. Traditions are also enthusiastically preserved with annual events such as the Nidderdale Festival and the Agricultural Show, one of the country's finest.

Little wonder then that Nidderdale is increasingly becoming more people's chosen destination and a mecca for walkers, mountain bikers and horseriders. A wide variety of additional leisure pursuits are also catered for including watersports, fishing, pot-holing and rock climbing. Its numerous caravan sites can also accommodate those who enjoy camping. There are many places to visit during your stay. At the upper end of the Dale lies How Stean Gorge, an amazing limestone cleft, known locally as 'Little Switzerland'. Middale, near

Netscape: Nidderdale, Yorkshire Dales – What to See and Do

Back Forward Reload Home Search Guide Images Print Security Stop

Location: http://www.nidderdale.co.uk/attractions.htm

Summerbridge, gaze upon the country's most awe-inspiring rock formation at Brimham Rocks.

Standing sentinel at the lower end of the Dale is Ripley Castle, home to the Ingilby family since the 1320's.

A short distance from Pateley Bridge discover the enchanting underground world of <u>Stump Cross Caverns</u>, with its illuminated display of stalagmites and stalactites. Enjoy the riverside walk to Glasshouses Mill and <u>Yorkshire Country Wines</u> to sample the delightful range of fruit wines produced in their vaulted cellars.

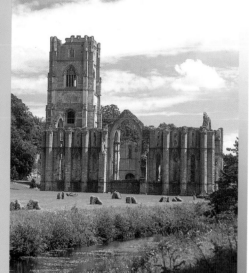

A little further afield, no visit would be complete without seeing the World Heritage site of Fountains Abbey and Studley Royal, widely regarded as the finest Cistercian monastic ruin in Europe.

Other favourites easily accessible from Nidderdale are the abbeys of Bolton and Jervaulx, the Bronte Parsonage at Howarth, Lightwater Valley Theme Park, and Masham's old established breweries.

Nidderdale – naturally a better place!

See also the maps of Nidderdale

© Nidderdale Chamber of Trade, 1999

WORD BANK

mecca a place which attracts people of a particular group

middale in the middle of the dale

sentinel a sentry or lookout

stalagmites shapes rising from the floor of a cave deposited by dripping water

stalactites shapes hanging from the roof of a cave formed by dripping water

Comparison

1 What phrase tells us that Pateley Bridge is an important town in this area?

2 What would you find near Summerbridge?

3 How many sports are advertised as available in Nidderdale? List them.

4 Text A is an autobiographical piece: the writer can say what he thinks and explain how he feels. Text B is different: it tries to tempt you to visit the place, so the language has been carefully chosen to give a particular impression of this part of Yorkshire.

Find ten adjectives in Text B, and then look back at the list of adjectives you found in Text A (Language question 1).
a) What do you notice about the adjectives used in each text?
b) Which adjectives are more positive and persuasive?
c) Which text is probably the most honest and reliable?

You should now be able to see that adjectives can be used in different ways depending on the purpose (the reason the text has been produced).

5 Refer back to the extract from Text A that you rewrote without adjectives (Language question 3).
a) Take the first paragraph of this article (Text B). Rewrite it, again removing the persuasive adjectives.
b) Would you be persuaded to go to Nidderdale based on your new version? Explain your answer in a sentence.
c) Your new version should become purely factual. List two of the facts in the paragraph.

6 You should now see that the persuasive adjectives are opinions, e.g. who is to say that the tea-rooms are 'cosy'? It is one person's opinion. Look at the extracts from the website on the next page. In each one, find one fact and one opinion.
Note: a fact is something that is true. An opinion is not true but one person's point of view.

A wide variety of additional leisure pursuits are also catered for...

Gaze upon the country's most awe-inspiring rock formation at Brimham Rocks...

Discover the enchanting underground world of Stump Cross Caverns...

Sample the delightful range of fruit wines produced in their vaulted cellars...

Fountains Abbey and Studley Royal, widely regarded as the finest Cistercian monastic ruin in Europe...

Writing assignments

1 If you were asked to produce an autobiographical piece on an event in your life, what would you choose? Write about one event in detail. You should:

- explain when and where it happened, and who was involved
- use vivid language (including adjectives) to create strong impressions of people and places
- use the first person singular 'I' and 'me' but avoid repeating them too much – experiment with different ways of helping your readers to see events, people and places through your eyes
- think about using dialogue to show what was said.

2 Design an Internet web page, advertising a holiday to the moon. You will need to:

- remember that all age groups could read this
- think about layout and how to present the page
- decide on key areas to include and links to other areas on the website
- use language positively, especially adjectives, to persuade your audience to book now – mix fact with opinion
- include pictures or photographs to link with the text
- aim to keep your writing short and concise – don't ramble on too much.

You could start like this:

> What better way to relax than a spectacular visit to the moon, set in the peaceful surroundings of wonderful outer space?

3 Each of you travels to school in some way every day. Write a short descriptive passage about a particular morning's journey. Think about how you travel to school, what you see on the way and what is around you. Remember to:

▶ choose words which will show your reader clearly what you saw and how you felt that day – use adjectives as in Text A to describe your surroundings

▶ don't just write down what you could see; include what you could hear, smell, taste or feel – use all your senses

▶ write in the first person singular, using 'I', but try to avoid starting each sentence in the same way.

You might begin:

> As usual, the groggy bus departed from my stop passing lush green fields and picturesque meadows.

Drama
Introducing characters

Aims

In this unit you will:

▶ study an extract from a playscript by a major dramatist

▶ learn about the ways in which a playwright introduces characters – before they appear on stage, and afterwards

▶ study another extract, this time from a TV situation comedy

▶ have a go at writing your own short script introducing a new character; turn a script into an extract from a novel; and write a letter of complaint.

Language focus

In this unit you will look at how playwrights and scriptwriters present characters. When we talk about characterization we mean everything that goes into creating a full and rounded description of a character – what they look like, what they think, say and do, and how they get on with other people.

Playwrights can give us an idea of what characters are like by having other characters tell us about them, before we see them on the stage.

Once the character has actually appeared on stage, the playwright can show characterization through dialogue and through stage directions.

> **Dialogue**
> Dialogue is the words spoken by the characters in the play. The sort of language characters use can tell us a lot about them:
> ▶ Is it formal or informal? Do they use slang?
> ▶ Are the sentences long or short?
> ▶ Do they speak with a particular accent or dialect?

Stage directions

Stage directions are instructions to the actor on **how** to speak or move on stage, and what emotions to show.

Short stage directions give instructions on how actors should say the lines. Often these directions are adverbs (e.g. timidly, angrily, confidently). Adverbs give additional information about verbs and usually end in -ly.

Longer stage directions allow the playwright to explain how characters look, how they are dressed, how they move and speak, etc. They use lots of adjectives. Adjectives are describing words that give us additional information about places, people, qualities, or ideas. Bernard Shaw, the playwright you are about to meet, is famous for writing long and very detailed stage directions full of adjectives.

TEXT A

George Bernard Shaw was born in Dublin in 1856. He moved to England in 1876 where he became very involved in socialist politics. At first he tried his hand at writing novels but these were not very successful. Instead, he turned to playscripts, using the stage to present and discuss ideas that interested him and expose those that he disapproved of. He died in 1950. He is now considered to be one of the most important dramatists of the twentieth century. Several of his plays have been adapted for television and made into films (including *St Joan*), and *Pygmalion* inspired the popular musical *My Fair Lady*.

Style note: Shaw believed that apostrophes served little use and purpose in most words, so he left them out – as in arent and thats.

St Joan is based on the true story of Joan of Arc. She was born in 1412 in a village in northeast France called Domrémy. Her father was a farmer and one of the headmen of his village. Joan's family was not rich and Joan worked on the farm, but they were not poor either. At the age of 13, she claimed to hear the voices of St Michael, St Catherine and St Margaret (the patron saints of France). They instructed Joan to dress as a man, become a soldier and lead the armies of France against the English invaders. Joan's first convert was a neighbouring squire...

SAINT JOAN

SCENE I

A fine spring morning on the river Meuse, between Lorraine and Champagne, in the year 1429 A.D., in the castle of Vaucouleurs.

Captain Robert de Baudricourt, a military squire, handsome and physically energetic, but with no will of his own, is disguising that defect in his usual fashion by storming terribly at his steward, a trodden worm, scanty of flesh, scanty of hair, who might be any age from 18 to 55, being the sort of man whom age cannot wither because he has never bloomed.

The two are in a sunny stone chamber on the first floor of the castle. At a plain strong oak table, seated in a chair to match, the captain presents his left profile. The steward stands facing him at the other side of the table, if so deprecatory a stance as his can be called standing. The mullioned thirteenth-century window is open behind him. Near it in the corner is a turret with a narrow arched doorway leading to a winding stair which descends to the courtyard. There is a stout fourlegged stool under the table, and a wooden chest under the window.

Robert	No eggs! No eggs!! Thousand thunders, man, what do you mean by no eggs?
Steward	Sir: it is not my fault. It is the act of God.
Robert	Blasphemy. You tell me there are no eggs; and you blame your Maker for it.
Steward	Sir: what can I do? I cannot lay eggs.
Robert	[*sarcastic*] Ha! You jest about it.
Steward	No, sir, God knows. We all have to go without eggs just as you have, sir. The hens will not lay.
Robert	Indeed! [*Rising*] Now listen to me, you.
Steward	[*humbly*] Yes, sir.
Robert	What am I?
Steward	What are you, sir?
Robert	[*coming at him*] Yes: what am I? Am I Robert, squire of Baudricourt and captain of this castle of Vaucouleurs; or am I a cowboy?

5

10

15

Steward	Oh, sir, you know you are a greater man here than the king himself.	
Robert	Precisely. And now, do you know what you are?	
Steward	I am nobody, sir, except that I have the honour to be your steward.	
Robert	[*driving him to the wall, adjective by adjective*] You have not only the honour of being my steward, but the privilege of being the worst, most incompetent, drivelling snivelling jibbering jabbering idiot of a steward in France. [*He strides back to the table.*]	20
Steward	[*cowering on the chest*] Yes, sir: to a great man like you I must seem like that.	
Robert	[*turning*] My fault, I suppose. Eh?	25
Steward	[*coming to him deprecatingly*] Oh, sir: you always give my most innocent words such a turn!	
Robert	I will give your neck a turn if you dare tell me, when I ask you how many eggs there are, that you cannot lay any.	
Steward	[*protesting*] Oh sir, oh sir –	30
Robert	No: not oh sir, oh sir, but no sir, no sir. My three Barbary hens and the black are the best layers in Champagne. And you come and tell me that there are no eggs! Who stole them? Tell me that, before I kick you out through the castle gate for a liar and a seller of my goods to thieves. The milk was short yesterday, too: do not forget that.	35
Steward	[*desperate*] I know, sir. I know only too well. There is no milk: there are no eggs: tomorrow there will be nothing.	
Robert	Nothing! You will steal the lot: eh?	
Steward	No, sir: nobody will steal anything. But there is a spell on us: we are bewitched.	40
Robert	That story is not good enough for me. Robert de Baudricourt burns witches and hangs thieves. Go. Bring me four dozen eggs and two gallons of milk here in this room before noon, or Heaven have mercy on your bones! I will teach you to make a fool of me. [*He resumes his seat with an air of finality.*]	45
Steward	Sir: I tell you there are no eggs. There will be none – not if you were to kill me for it – as long as The Maid is at the door.	
Robert	The Maid! What maid? What are you talking about?	
Steward	The girl from Lorraine, sir. From Domrémy.	

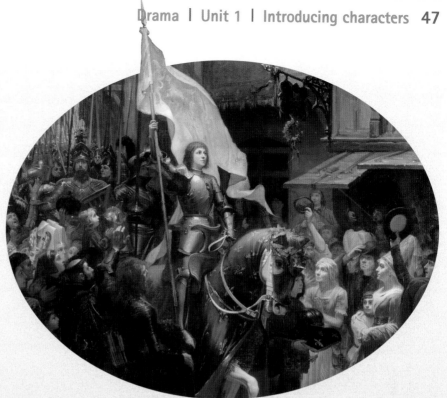

Robert	[*rising in fearful wrath*] Thirty thousand thunders! Fifty thousand devils! Do you mean to say that that girl, who had the impudence to ask to see me two days ago, and whom I told you to send back to her father with my orders that he was to give her a good hiding, is here still?	50
Steward	I have told her to go, sir. She wont.	55
Robert	I did not tell you to tell her to go: I told you to throw her out. You have fifty men-at-arms and a dozen lumps of able-bodied servants to carry out my orders. Are they afraid of her?	
Steward	She is so positive, sir.	
Robert	[*seizing him by the scruff of the neck*] Positive! Now see here. I am going to throw you downstairs.	60
Steward	No, sir. Please.	
Robert	Well, stop me by being positive. It's quite easy: any slut of a girl can do it.	
Steward	[*hanging limp in his hands*] Sir, sir: you cannot get rid of her by throwing me out. [*Robert has to let him drop. He squats on his knees on the floor, contemplating his master resignedly.*] You see, sir, you are much more positive than I am. But so is she.	65
Robert	I am stronger than you are, you fool.	
Steward	No, sir. It isnt that: it's your strong character, sir. She is weaker than we are: she is only a slip of a girl; but we cannot make her go.	70

Robert	You parcel of curs: you are afraid of her.
Steward	[*rising cautiously*] No sir: we are afraid of you; but she puts courage into us. She really doesnt seem to be afraid of anything. Perhaps you could frighten her, sir.

75

Robert	[*grimly*] Perhaps. Where is she now?
Steward	Down in the courtyard, sir, talking to the soldiers as usual. She is always talking to the soldiers except when she is praying.
Robert	Praying! Ha! You believe she prays, you idiot. I know the sort of girl that is always talking to soldiers. She shall talk to me a bit. [*He goes to the window and shouts fiercely through it*] Hallo, you there!

80

A girl's voice	[*bright, strong, and rough*] Is it me, sir?
Robert	Yes, you.
The voice	Be you captain?
Robert	Yes, damn your impudence, I be captain. Come up here. [*To the soldiers in the yard*] Show her the way, you. And shove her along quick. [*He leaves the window, and returns to his place at the table, where he sits magisterially.*]

85

Steward	[*whispering*] She wants to go and be a soldier herself. She wants you to give her soldier's clothes. Armour, sir! And a sword! Actually! [*He steals behind Robert.*]

90

Joan appears in the turret doorway. She is an ablebodied country girl of 17 or 18, respectably dressed in red, with an uncommon face; eyes very wide apart and bulging as they often do in very imaginative people, a long well-shaped nose with wide nostrils, a short upper lip, resolute but full-lipped mouth, and handsome fighting chin. She comes eagerly to the table, delighted at having penetrated to Baudricourt's presence at last, and full of hope as to the result. His scowl does not check or frighten her in the least. Her voice is normally a hearty coaxing voice, very confident, very appealing, very hard to resist.

Joan	[*bobbing a curtsey*] Good morning, captain squire. Captain: you are to give me a horse and armour and some soldiers, and send me to the Dauphin. Those are your orders from my Lord.
Robert	[*outraged*] Orders from your lord! And who the devil may your lord be? Go back to him, and tell him that I am neither duke nor peer at his orders: I am squire of Baudricourt; and I take no orders except from the king.

95

Joan	[*reassuringly*] Yes, squire: that is all right. My Lord is the King of Heaven.	100
Robert	Why, the girl's mad. [*To the steward*] Why didn't you tell me so, you blockhead?	
Steward	Sir: do not anger her: give her what she wants.	
Joan	[*impatient, but friendly*] They all say I am mad until I talk to them, squire. But you see that it is the will of God that you are to do what He has put into my mind.	105
Robert	It is the will of God that I shall send you back to your father with orders to put you under lock and key and thrash the madness out of you. What have you to say to that?	
Joan	You think you will, squire; but you will find it all coming quite different. You said you would not see me; but here I am.	110
Steward	[*appealing*] Yes, sir. You see, sir.	
Robert	Hold your tongue, you.	
Steward	[*abjectly*] Yes, sir.	
Robert	[*to Joan, with a sour loss of confidence*] So you are presuming on my seeing you, are you?	115
Joan	[*sweetly*] Yes, squire.	
Robert	[*feeling that he has lost ground, brings down his two fists squarely on the table, and inflates his chest imposingly to cure the unwelcome and only too familiar sensation*] Now listen to me. I am going to assert myself.	120
Joan	[*busily*] Please do, squire. The horse will cost sixteen francs. It is a good deal of money: but I can save it on the armour. I can find a soldier's armour that will fit me well enough: I am very hardy; and I do not need beautiful armour made to my measure like you wear. I shall not want many soldiers: the Dauphin will give me all I need to raise the siege of Orleans.	125
Robert	[*flabbergasted*] To raise the siege of Orleans!	
Joan	[*simply*] Yes, squire: that is what God is sending me to do. Three men will be enough for you to send with me if they are good men and gentle to me. They have promised to come with me. Polly and Jack and –	130
Robert	Polly!! You impudent baggage, do you dare call squire Bertrand de Poulengey Polly to my face?	
Joan	His friends call him so, squire: I did not know he had any other name. Jack –	135

Robert	That is Monsieur John of Metz, I suppose?
Joan	Yes, squire. Jack will come willingly: he is a very kind gentleman, and gives me money to give to the poor. I think John Godsave will come, and Dick the Archer, and their servants John of Honecourt and Julian. There will be no trouble for you, squire: I have arranged it all: you have only to give the order.

140

Robert	[*contemplating her in a stupor of amazement*] Well, I am damned!
Joan	[*with unruffled sweetness*] No, squire: God is very merciful; and the blessed saints Catherine and Margaret, who speak to me every day [*he gapes*], will intercede for you. You will go to paradise; and your name will be remembered for ever as my first helper.

145

Robert	[*to the steward, still much bothered, but changing his tone as he pursues a new clue*] Is this true about Monsieur de Poulengey?
Steward	[*eagerly*] Yes, sir, and about Monsieur de Metz too. They both want to go with her.

150

Robert	[*thoughtful*] Mf! [*He goes to the window, and shouts into the courtyard*] Hallo! You there: send Monsieur de Poulengey to me, will you? [*He turns to Joan*] Get out; and wait in the yard.
Joan	[*smiling brightly at him*] Right, squire. [*She goes out.*]
Robert	[*to the steward*] Go with her, you, you dithering imbecile. Stay within call; and keep your eye on her. I shall have her up here again.

155

Steward   Do so in God's name, sir. Think of those hens, the best layers in Champagne; and –

Robert   Think of my boot; and take your backside out of reach of it.

George Bernard Shaw

WORD BANK

abjectly humbly

age cannot wither because he has never bloomed has looked old and tired since the day he was born

Barbary hens hens from north Africa

blasphemy speaking in a way that is disrespectful or offensive about God

Dauphin the eldest son of the French King; here the Dauphin is actually the king, but due to the wars with the English, he has not been crowned

francs the currency used in France

imposingly in a way to inspire fear or respect

impudent baggage a cheeky young woman

Lorraine/Champagne areas of northeast France

mullioned a type of window

peer a person of noble birth, like a lord

scanty of flesh skinny, thin

scanty of hair with very little hair

siege of Orleans Orleans is a city in northern France. The English have surrounded it. Joan has been told by her voices to help defeat the English and liberate Orleans.

so deprecatory a stance the way the steward stands, suggesting he feels humble and apologetic

squire a landowner, usually of noble birth

steward a higher servant who organizes the everyday running of a castle and gives orders to others working for the squire

storming terribly shouting in a loud and frightening way

turret a small tower on a medieval castle

Language questions

1   Draw a table with three columns, like this:

Robert	Steward	Joan

Under each heading, pick out the adjectives used in the stage directions to tell us about the personality of each character.

Then pick out the adverbs which describe how each character speaks and the things they do.

Can you find other descriptive words within the stage directions which don't end in *ly*? Write these down in the appropriate column and see if you can change them into adverbs. For example: in Robert's column, 'sarcastic' will become 'sarcastically'.

You may find you need to look up some of these words in a dictionary to be sure of their meanings.

2 Look at this example of lines spoken by Robert de Baudricourt (lines 50–54).

Robert	[*rising in fearful wrath*] Thirty thousand thunders! Fifty thousand devils! Do you mean to say that that girl, who had the impudence to ask to see me two days ago, and whom I told you to send back to her father with my orders that he was to give her a good hiding, is still here?

What do these lines tell us about the character of Robert? It may help you to think about:

▸ the person he is speaking to and the relationship he has with that person
▸ what he actually says and how he says it
▸ the sentences – are they short or long, simple or complex?
▸ the vocabulary – is it easy to understand or are there any words you need to look up in a dictionary?
▸ the punctuation – particularly exclamation marks and question marks.

Then write a short paragraph on what you can tell about Robert from what he says and the way he speaks.

3 Now look at this line spoken by the steward (line 3).

Steward	Sir: it is not my fault. It is the act of God.

What does this line tell you about the character of the steward? It may help to think about:

- the person he is speaking to and the relationship he has with that person
- what he actually says and how he says it
- the sentences – are they short or long, simple or complex?
- the vocabulary – is it easy to understand or are there any words you need to look up in a dictionary?
- the punctuation – particularly the lack of exclamation marks.

4 Finally, read these lines spoken by Joan (line 84, lines 92–94).

Joan Be you captain?

Joan [*bobbing a curtsey*] Good morning, captain squire. Captain: you are to give me a horse and armour and some soldiers, and send me to the Dauphin. Those are your orders from my Lord.

What do these lines tell you about the character of Joan? It may help to think about:

- the person she is speaking to and the relationship she has with that person
- what she actually says and how she says it
- the sentences – are they short or long, simple or complex?
- the vocabulary – is it easy to understand or are there any words you need to look up in a dictionary?
- the punctuation – particularly the commas and the colons, and the absence of questions.

Comprehension

1 Where and in what year is this first scene set?

2 According to the steward, what two things does Joan spend her time doing while she waits to see Robert de Baudricourt?

3 Who tells Robert that he has orders from God? What are these orders?

4 What does Robert mean when he says: 'I am going to assert myself' (line 120)? What does Joan think he means?

5 When Joan calls Bertrand de Poulengey 'Polly', Robert is shocked. Why do you think this is?

6 Copy out these statements and write true or false against them.

▶ Robert de Baudricourt bullies his steward.
▶ The steward persuades Robert to send Joan packing.
▶ Joan has convinced several experienced soldiers to support her.
▶ The steward thinks that Joan has special powers.
▶ Joan is frightened of Robert de Baudricourt.
▶ Joan is vain and asks for a beautiful suit of armour.
▶ Robert de Baudricourt has met his match with Joan.

7 a) Write down three facts you have learned about Joan before she enters.
b) What does Robert de Baudricourt think of Joan before he meets her?
c) What does the steward think of her?

8 There are three characters in this scene – which one do you like most and why? Which do you like least? Draw two examples from the play for each character, to support your argument.

9 Joan's story is tragic. She fights in bloody battles, is betrayed by her countrymen, and condemned to death by the English.
a) Do you think any of this extract is funny?
b) Pick out what you consider to be the funniest line or speech from the text. Explain your choice in a short paragraph.
c) Pick out the funniest action from the extract. Explain your choice in a short paragraph.
d) On the evidence of this extract, do you think this play will be mainly funny, mainly sad, or a mixture of both?

Speaking and listening

1

Groups/pairs

In groups, brainstorm your thoughts on

▶ the character of the steward
▶ his opinion of his master, Robert de Baudricourt
▶ his view of Joan.

Then, imagine that you are a distant cousin of the steward. You don't see him very often, but your work has brought you within a mile of the castle at Vaucouleurs. You decide to pay your cousin a call. You have heard that Robert de Baudricourt has a reputation as a bad-tempered bully and you have also heard some strange stories about a young country girl who dresses as a man.

In groups, brainstorm some of the questions you might want to ask the steward, about

▶ his work
▶ his boss
▶ the girl.

Working in pairs, role play a conversation between the steward and his cousin. The steward is keen to retell the events of Text A from his point of view. He also has some things to say about Robert de Baudricourt and Joan. The cousin is interested in any kind of gossip and has many questions to ask. Share some of these improvisations with the rest of the class.

2

Groups

Improvise the scene between Joan and Robert's soldiers in the courtyard of the castle.

Work in groups of four or five people. Think carefully about the characterization of Joan and the soldiers before you start. Fill in a 'character card' for each person involved in the scene. You could set it out like the examples on the next page.

Name: Joan the maid
Age:
Appearance:
Personality:
Reason for being in the courtyard:
What she wants to say to the soldiers:
How she plans to say it:
Her hopes and fears:

Name: Peter – a soldier
Age:
Appearance:
Personality:
Opinion of Joan:
Opinion of Robert de Baudricourt:
For Joan or against her?

Try to create three or four very different characters for the soldiers – aim for a variety of ages, personalities and opinions.

Allocate the roles.

To get into your character, you may want to try a short hot-seating exercise.

Each member of the group should take the hot seat in role as their chosen character. Set a time limit of 2-3 minutes. During that time, the rest of the group should ask rapid questions to find out as much information as possible about the character in the hot seat.

Now improvise the scene in the castle courtyard. Joan is sitting waiting to see Robert. She has been waiting for two days. A group of soldiers enter.

You could end the scene when Joan goes into the castle to see Robert.

TEXT B

Here is another passage from a script – this time a TV script – showing the introduction of a new character. It is taken from *The Vicar of Dibley* by Richard Curtis, who also wrote *Blackadder*, *Mr Bean*, and the film scripts for *Four Weddings and a Funeral* and *Notting Hill*.

This extract does not come at the beginning of the drama so it will help if we set the scene.

The elderly vicar of Dibley, the Reverend Pottle, has died. Members of the parish council are gathered at Dibley Manor (home of David Horton, the chairman of the parish council) to welcome 'the new chap' who is to be his replacement.

Note: TV scripts do not use long stage directions to say what characters look like and how they behave. In fact, the only information about a character so far in the script is that David Horton is 'an intolerant 50 year old country squire'. Characterization in this script is through words and actions.

The Vicar of Dibley

<u>7. – INT – DAVID'S LIVING ROOM – NIGHT</u>
A SHOT OF DAVID POURING SHERRY LINKS US BACK INTO THE LIVING ROOM AGAIN – IT IS A STORMY NIGHT, THE NEXT WEEKEND

ALICE
(OOV) O, sherry – wow!

DAVID
Only the best here, Miss Tinker.

ALICE
Thank you very much.

MRS CROPLEY
Sandwich?

DAVID
No thank you. Anchovy and peanut butter not quite my cup of tea. Frank, sherry?

FRANK
O thank you very much – lovely – my favourite.

DAVID
There we are. Jim?

JIM
No, no, no, no, no, no – yes.

DAVID
There we are. Don't drink it all at once – top stuff. (COUGHS.) As you all know we're all gathered here to greet our new vicar. I'm sorry it's such an awful night. I can't fix everything.

THEY ALL LAUGH.

HUGO
Though, you did get our cat fixed, didn't you.

HE LAUGHS NERVOUSLY. THE DOORBELL GOES.

DAVID
I think our new vicar has arrived. Either that or the milkman's very late again.

THEY ALL LAUGH NERVOUSLY.

8. – EXT – DAVID'S HALL/FRONT DOOR – NIGHT
WE SEE A BRIGHT YELLOW FIGURE, KNOCKING, AND PRESSING HER FACE AGAINST THE GLASS.

GERALDINE
Hello. Hello. Sorry – could you hurry – it's pissing down out here. Raining very hard now. Please.

DAVID OPENS THE DOOR. IT IS A CHEERFUL 35 YEAR OLD LADY IN FULL YELLOW PLASTIC RAIN GEAR. HER NAME IS GERALDINE. SHE HOLDS TWO BAGS.

GERALDINE
Hello. David – Honiton? Hawtrey?

DAVID
Horton.

GERALDINE
Horton. That's the chap. Could you just… take these while I…

SHE MOVES BACK TO CAB AND PICKS UP TWO MORE BAGS.

GERALDINE
Cheers. Bye.

GOES BACK INTO HOUSE

GERALDINE
Excuse me. Just get past you. Thank you.

8A – INT – DAVID'S HALL – NIGHT

GERALDINE
Hello. I'm Geraldine. I believe you're expecting me.

DAVID
No, I'm expecting our new vicar. Unless, of course, you are the new vicar and they've landed us with a woman as some sort of insane joke.

SHE MEANWHILE TAKES OFF HER MAC. HE IS STUNNED BY THE TRUTH.

GERALDINE
Oh dear.

DAVID
Oh my god.

GERALDINE
You were expecting a bloke – beard, bible… bad breath…

DAVID
Yes, that sort of thing.

GERALDINE
Yeah. And, instead you've got a babe with a bob cut and a magnificent bosom.

DAVID
So I see.

GERALDINE
Well, don't worry. It'll be all right. You need a stiff drink. So do I. Come on David.

HUGO COMES INTO THE HALL TO SEE WHAT'S UP.

GERALDINE
Hullo, I'm Geraldine, call me Gerry.

HUGO
Delighted to meet you. I'm Hugo. Call me Hugo.

GERALDINE
Right. Do you mind if I say that's a devastatingly smart tie, Hugo.

HUGO
Is it.

GERALDINE
Yeah. Shall we go in there.

THEY MOVE INTO LOUNGE.

9. – INT – DAVID'S LIVING ROOM – NIGHT

DAVID
Ladies and gentlemen… your new vicar.

GERALDINE
Hullo – Geraldine (MRS CROPLEY/FRANK/ALICE STARE) Boo.

FRANK
How do you do – I'm Frank Pickle. I take the minutes on the Council.

GERALDINE
Splendid. Very important job. Do forgive me if I instantly forget your name won't you. I'm absolutely dreadful with names. Ask me to name the Virgin Mary's eldest son, and nope – mind's gone blank.

FRANK
Jesus.

GERALDINE
That's it. Yes.

GERALDINE
Hullo, Geraldine. Gerry.

MRS CROPLEY
Letitia… Letty. Cropley. I do the flowers in the church.

GERALDINE
O splendid. And what have we got in this week?

MRS CROPLEY
Oh well, we're in mourning for Reverend Pottle.

GERALDINE
Of course. Lovely. Carnations.

MRS CROPLEY
Yes. And I thought I'd put in a pineapple as well.

GERALDINE
(PAUSE) Unusual. And you are?

JIM
No, no, no, no, Jim.

GERALDINE
Jim?

JIM
No, no, no, no…

GERALDINE
Not Jim.

JIM
No, no, no – yes, Jim.

GERALDINE
Good. Good. And finally…

ALICE
Delighted to meet you.

DAVID
This is Miss Tinker, she <u>was</u> the verger under Reverend Pottle.

GERALDINE
Oh, splendid. Do you want to go on with the job?

ALICE
Oh, yes please, Ma'am. I'd like to.

DAVID IN SHOCK.

GERALDINE
Good. Good. Don't call me 'Ma'am', sounds like the Queen. Lovely lady – but very odd taste in hats. Don't you think so – Miss Tinker?

ALICE
Yes I do.

GERALDINE
Yes. Yes. Yes.

ALICE
Oh you can call me Alice.

GERALDINE
Right.

ALICE
Because it's my name.

GERALDINE
Right.

DAVID
Perhaps we should talk about all this in the morning.

HE OFFERS HER A SHERRY.

GERALDINE
Yes. Thanks. Ugh. Oo. Do you mind – absolutely hate Amontillado. You wouldn't have any whisky would you?

DAVID
Ahm, certainly, ahm, yes.

HE SNEAKS TO THE CUPBOARD, SECRETIVELY TO POUR HER ONE DRINK.

FRANK
I wouldn't mind a whisky, if there's any going.

MRS CROPLEY
Me too.

DAVID
(WEARY) Jim?

JIM
No, no, no, no, no…

DAVID
Please yourself…

JIM
Yes. I'll have a whisky.

(DOORBELL)

GERALDINE
Very unusual sandwiches. What's this with the ham?

MRS CROPLEY
Lemon curd.

GERALDINE
Good lord. Mind if I just pop it down there. Just for a moment. I'd like to say a big thank you to all of you for coming along on such a horrible night, when you could be in watching (CHECKS WATCH) Ooo, Top of the Pops. We're missing Top of the Pops. Anyway, here's cheers.

ENTER NEWITT

NEWITT
Sorry I'm late. I've been on the kasi since sundown.

DAVID
Ah, Owen – this is Geraldine – she's the new vicar.

GERALDINE
Hello.

NEWITT
No she isn't.

GERALDINE
Why not?

NEWITT
She's a woman.

Richard Curtis

Comparison

1 *The Vicar of Dibley* is a television script and is therefore set out in a different way to *St Joan* which is a stage play. How many differences can you find in the way the script is set out on the page? You could look at:

▶ breaks between the action
▶ vocabulary used in stage directions
▶ characters' names.

2 Copy out columns one and two from the table below. Then find examples from the script that back up the comments in column two and add them to column three.

Name of character	Personality traits	Evidence from the script that backs this up (one or two examples)
David Horton	intolerant; has strong opinions	
Hugo Horton	pleasant, but not very clever	
Frank Pickle	quite proper, not much sense of humour	
Jim Trot	starts every sentence with 'no' even when he means 'yes'	
Letitia Cropley	has strange tastes in sandwich fillings and flower arrrangements	
Owen Newitt	has stomach problems and likes to tell people about them	
Alice Tinker	very naïve, seems not quite 'all there'	
Geraldine Granger	not at all traditional, outspoken	

3 Look back at Text A at the stage directions that Shaw wrote to introduce the character of Joan. Now write a similar stage direction for the actor playing Geraldine to show what her character is like. Aim for between 50 and 75 words.

4 a) Which of the following adjectives do you think best describe Geraldine?

▶ friendly   ▶ jokey
▶ nervous   ▶ disrespectful
▶ cheerful   ▶ shy
▶ enthusiastic   ▶ rude
▶ thoughtful

Can you add any of your own to this list?

b) Now find three things Geraldine says which you would not expect a vicar to say. Write a couple of sentences to explain each choice.

5 Both George Bernard Shaw and Richard Curtis have a number of ways of showing their audience what the characters in their scripts are like. List the different techniques they use. Then find an example of each technique from Text A and Text B.

Writing assignments

1 Re-write either Text A or Text B as the beginning of a novel. Before you start, you need to think carefully about the following things:

▶ Decide on which narrative viewpoint you will use. If you choose to write in the first person this means writing from the point of view of one of the characters in the scene, e.g.:

It was raining when I arrived...

This can be more personal and immediate. Third person ('he' or 'she') is perhaps less personal, but it will allow you to describe events from the point of view of more than one character.

▶ Use the information about places and people from the stage directions, but don't just copy out chunks of stage direction into your novel opening. Write your story in your own style. You may want to add further information and descriptions of your own. This will certainly be the case if you choose Text B which has very few stage directions.

▶ Remember, if you decide to put the dialogue into direct speech you will need to use speech marks. Again, don't feel you have to use every bit of dialogue from the script in your story.

▶ Think about the beginning and the end of your passage. A gripping opening will immediately capture the reader's attention and a satisfying ending will leave the reader wanting to find out more.

▶ Include the private thoughts and feelings of the characters – something you can't easily do in a play or TV script.

2 Write a scene for a playscript about the arrival of a new character. You could choose one of the three starting points below.

> A A single dad brings home his new girlfriend to meet his children.
>
> B A strange new pupil arrives at school. He/she is an alien in disguise.
>
> C A famous sports star or singer is expected at a fundraising event.

You will need to think about:
▶ who you want in your play
▶ how you will set it out
▶ what other characters say before the new arrival appears
▶ information about the new arrival in the form of stage directions
▶ what we learn about the character from his/her own actions and words.

3 Imagine you are David Horton. Write a letter to the Bishop of Wykeham explaining why Geraldine cannot remain in her post as Vicar of Dibley.

You should include:

▶ David's opinion of women vicars in general

▶ David's opinion of Geraldine in particular

▶ the views of other people in Dibley about these points.

You will find plenty of evidence to help you in Text B. However, you may also find these comments from other parts of the script helpful.

David Horton

I won't have my village used like some laboratory animal to see if women vicars 'work'.

If Jesus wanted women to spread the gospel he would have appointed them. It's Matthew, Mark, Luke and John – not Sharon, Tracy, Tara, and Debbie.

I think you will find that our little community does not react well to the indignity of a vicar in high heels and rallies behind me in the desire to keep up with the traditions that have made this village and the Church of England what they are today.

Owen Newitt

Well it can't be right, can it really? Having a woman vicar. I mean, Jesus didn't have women disciples, did he?

Remember: you are writing this letter as David Horton. It should be set out as a formal letter and written in paragraphs. You will probably want to use a formal style. You should introduce the 'problem', explain why it is a problem and suggest a solution.

Drama
The power of speech

Aims

In this unit you will:

- study an extract from a playscript adapted from a contemporary novel for children
- look at aspects of informal spoken English and see how and why this is used in playscript dialogue
- focus on the features of Australian dialect
- study a poem by a living major poet on a similar theme
- write a play extract, newspaper article or essay based on the texts you have read.

Language focus

The extract you are about to read is set in Australia. The hero, Colin, speaks in a very informal way. His speech is also peppered with Australian slang.

Look at the opening dialogue between Colin and his mum, which shows several features of informal speech:

Colin	Morning Mum. Gor, you sure you're packin enough? They've probly got a kitchen sink in Sydney, you know.
Mum	This is not for Sydney.
Colin	But them's my clothes.

Features of informal speech

Feature	Example	Formal version
Missing letters	packin probly	pack<u>ing</u> prob<u>ab</u>ly
'Ungrammatical' sentences	'Morning' 'You sure you're packin enough?' 'Them's my clothes'	'<u>Good</u> morning' '<u>Are</u> you sure you're packing enough?' '<u>Those are</u> my clothes'
Elided words (two words joined together)	you're packin they've	<u>you are</u> packing <u>they have</u>

All these features make Colin sound like a real teenager, having a real conversation with his mum. Spellings like 'packin' and 'probly' also tell the actor how to pronounce the words in the way that Colin would.

Australian slang and dialect
Dialect is vocabulary and language structures which are used by people from a particular region. Colin (and other characters in this playscript) speak in Australian dialect which has different vocabulary and grammar to standard English, e.g.:

Standard English	Australian dialect
Hello	G'day

TEXT A

Morris Gleitzman was born in the UK, but moved to Australia with his family when he was 16. He began his writing career as a journalist and screenwriter before trying his hand at novels. He has written a number of books for children including *Two Weeks with the Queen, Misery Guts, Worry Warts, Blabber Mouth,*

and *Gift of the Gab*. His stories tackle tricky subjects – bullying, coping with disabilities, family problems, illness and death – with sensitivity, honesty and humour. He bounces his readers from tears to laughter.

Mary Morris, an Australian playwright, has adapted *Two Weeks with the Queen* for the stage. It was first performed in the UK by the Royal National Theatre.

Colin Mudford, the main character in *Two Weeks with the Queen*, lives with his mum, dad and younger brother Luke in Australia. On Christmas Day, Luke suddenly collapses. Colin assumes he has eaten too much Christmas dinner and has got 'gastric'. Luke is sent for tests in hospital; then suddenly Colin's parents make an announcement...

TWO WEEKS WITH THE QUEEN

Mum is carrying a bundle of Colin-size clothes. She starts folding them into a huge suitcase. Colin enters yawning.

Colin	Morning Mum. Gor, you sure you're packin enough? They've probly got a kitchen sink in Sydney, you know.
Mum	This is not for Sydney.
Colin	But them's my clothes.
Mum	Colin, your dad rung from the Sydney hospital last night. Him and me 5 ... We'd like you to go and stay with Uncle Bob and Auntie Iris in England for a bit.
Colin	Wha...?
Mum	We're not going to make you go. But we'd like you to. For your sake and for ours. 10
Colin	I can't go to England – cricket practice starts next week.
Mum	You'll have a great time over there. Uncle Bob and Auntie Iris live near London Zoo and Uncle Bob goes to the cricket all the time. And little Alistair, your cousin, he's practically your age.
Colin	What'd I do...? 15
Mum	Oh love, it's not that. It's just for the best. The doctors say Luke isn't going to get better.
Colin	From gastric? People always get better from gastric!

Mum	It's not gastric. They showed Dad the X-rays. It's... It's...
Colin	No! I can be a help to you! I can make the tea so you can look after him. I can bring him his homework from school. You don't have to send me away!
Mum	Colin, a terrible thing's happening and we don't want you to have to suffer too.
Colin	What terrible thing? What's so terrible you have to send me away?
Mum	Don't you understand! Luke's got cancer! He's going to die!

She rushes out. Colin shouts after her.

Colin	Bull! I don't believe you! They're bein' slack! If they can sew a bloke's foot on and put a new heart in somebody surely they can cure a bit of cancer! [*He starts to throw his clothes angrily out of the suitcase.*] What about the man in the newsagents? He had cancer on his head and they cured him. Expect me to believe that you can get the cricket from India and get bombs that could blow the whole world up and robots and space ships and they can't cure a bit of cancer! Bull! They're just not tryin'! [*He slumps down.*] Bloody slack. If it was somebody important they'd pull their finger out alright. If it was the Prime Minister they'd be askin' the Queen of England for the world's best doctor's phone number then, eh? I bet the Queen has the world's best doctor right there beside her in London. London! [*He starts throwing the clothes back in the suitcase. He picks it up and leaves the room.*] Hey Mum. What time's my plane?

Colin, Mum and Dad are waiting at the airport for the plane to board.

20

25

30

35

40

Colin	You don't have to worry. Everything's going to be OK.
Dad	Good on ya, Col.
Colin	No, I mean, Luke isn't going to die.
Dad	Don't son.
Colin	Mum, are you listening? I said, Luke isn't going to die. 45
Mum	[*sharply*] Don't talk about things you don't understand.
Colin	I do understand.
Dad	Colin, it's not up to us.
Colin	I know. That's what I'm trying to explain.
Mum	[*too brightly*] Why don't you think about all the exciting things you're 50 going to do with Uncle Bob and Auntie Iris and Alistair.
Colin	Stack me, some people don't want to be cheered up! Mum, I'm trying to tell you about Luke.
Mum	Don't talk about it. Please don't.

Dad takes him aside while Mum composes herself.

Dad	We've got to be strong old mate, and cop it on the chin. 55
Colin	But Dad...
Dad	Now, when you write to Luke, don't say anything about... You know.
Colin	The cancer.
Dad	The doctors haven't and we've decided not to. Don't want him scared on top of everything. 60
Colin	Don't worry, I won't say anything about him dying, cos he's not going to.
Mum	[*joining them again*] Be a good boy for Uncle Bob and Auntie Iris, won't you? It was kind of them to help out with the ticket and everything.
Colin	Yeh, yeh. 65

A flight attendant approaches.

Flight Att	Colin Mudford?
Mum	Yes, this is Colin.
Flight Att	I'm your flight attendant. I'll be looking after you on the plane.

Colin	Let's go.
Flight Att	We'll get you boarded then.
Mum	Oh, your passport – here, and some English money. It's not much, but...
Colin	I won't need much.
Mum	It's for the best, love. We'll send for you soon – once it's all... When it's all...
Dad	We'll leave you to it then, son.
Flight Att	Don't worry, we'll see him right.
Mum	And keep warm, won't you?

Colin embraces Mum.

Colin	[*to Dad*] Don't worry, I got it all worked out. I got a plan.
Loudspeaker Voice	This is your boarding call for Qantas flight number one to London via Melbourne and Singapore. Now boarding at gate ten, Qantas flight number one to London via Melbourne and Singapore.

The attendant takes Colin to his seat.

Flight Att	This is your call button. If you need a drink or anything, just press it. Someone will come round with headphones and there'll be a movie later.
Colin	This is great. How long is it?
Flight Att	Oh, twenty four hours or so.
Colin	No, the plane, not the flight.
Flight Att	Oh, sorry. [*She tells him in metres.*]
Colin	You know, that's long enough for an indoor cricket pitch. If you moved all the seats out down one side you could have one, then all your passengers would get the exercise which would counteract the effects of jet lag.
Flight Att	I'll pass that on to the Captain.

A grim-faced businessman rushes in late and sits beside Colin. The attendant goes through the usual vacuous safety routine to the unintelligible voice on the intercom. The noise of the plane taxi-ing for take-off is heard. Throughout the flight, the businessman tries to ignore Colin.

70

75

80

85

90

Colin [*to the businessman*] Lifejackets! Great. You think we better get ours   95
out? You'd be right. In the water, I mean. Got enough fat on you to
keep you warm. I'd be a gonner. [*The noise rises in pitch.*] Woa, some
speed eh? Did you know most plane crashes happen on take-off? [*They
lean back as the plane takes off.*] Hey, there's Sydney harbour bridge.
Isn't it beautiful? My brother's in Sydney, in hospital. You reckon   100
they're all lookin' up at us while we're lookin' down? I bet him and all
the nurses are lookin' out the hospital window at us. Wave, go on,
just in case. I bet he's ropable, he only got to go in the air ambulance,
I'm in a jumbo. Boo sucks Lukey mate!

Later.

Gor, they don't half feed you a lot. I'm as stuffed as a Christmas   105
turkey.

The businessman gives a grunt of pain.

Is that a bit of cancer?

Businessman I beg your pardon?

Colin Cancer. It's where the cells start growing too fast inside your body
and your whole system can go bung. I've been reading up on it.   110

Businessman I know what it is. I just don't particularly want to talk about it.

Colin Funny that. My folks are the same. Why not?

Businessman Because it's not a very pleasant topic.

Colin There's worse topics. [*He thinks.*] Like nuclear war and why sick has
bits in it. [*The businessman groans.*] Only, if you've got it, I'd have it   115
seen to.

Businessman I haven't got it! I've got indigestion.

Colin Mum always gets indigestion if she bolts her tucker.

Later.

You want a go at doing this quiz? Which Prime Minister played cricket
for Australia? No? Do you want to colour in this picture of a koala?   120
The crayons are a bit crappy but it was good of the Hostie to give it to
me.

The Captain and the attendant appear.

Captain	G'day Colin. Thought you might like a look at the flight deck.
Colin	Too right! [*He stands.*]
Businessman	Excuse me, Miss, do you have any other seats available?
Colin	Oh, don't worry. I'm going up to the flight deck, so you can have both seats for a while.
Captain	So. We're travelling to London by ourselves, eh?
Colin	Well, I am.
Captain	And what are you going to do in London?
Colin	I'm going to see the Queen.
Captain	The Queen, eh? [*He winks at the attendant.*] Going to drop in for tea and cucumber sandwiches are you?
Colin	No. I'm going to ask her to help cure my brother's cancer.
Captain	Ar, em, yes, well...

125

130

135

Mary Morris
adapted from the novel by Morris Gleitzman

WORD BANK

All the Australian slang words are explained in Language question 1.

composes herself gets her emotion under control

flight deck where the pilot sits in an aircraft

gate ten a numbered exit in a large airport, leading to the airfield

intercom a sound system for communicating to passengers in an aircraft

jet lag the feeling of tiredness experienced by air travellers who cross time zones on long distance flights

jumbo a jumbo-jet aircraft

kitchen sink this refers to the saying 'I've got everything in here bar/but the kitchen sink'; i.e. 'I've packed too many things'

koala a type of bear found in Australia

Melbourne second largest city in Australia

Qantas the name of the airline

Singapore an island in southeast Asia; often a stop-over for flights between Australia and London

Sydney the largest city in Australia (Luke is in hospital there)

Sydney harbour bridge a famous landmark in Sydney

taxi-ing describes the movement of an aircraft along the ground before take-off

unintelligible impossible to understand

vacuous mindless

Language questions

1 In column A there is a list of the Australian dialect words and grammar used in this extract. In column B is an explanation or alternative word in standard English. Match the Australian dialect word with the right word or groups of words in column B.

Column A	Column B
gor	'I don't believe it'
gastric	not doing their job properly
bull	'Good day' or a polite 'hello'
slack	full of food
good on ya	get blocked up
stack me	angry
cop it on the chin	useless, no good
ropable	eats her food too fast
stuffed	cor (an exclamation of surprise)
bung	air hostess or flight attendant
bolts her tucker	'I'd like that very much'
crappy	'good for you'
hostie	a stomach upset
G'day	like 'take it on the chin' (be brave)
too right	'that's rubbish'

2 Copy out the table below. Look at all the characters in Text A in turn and record any elided words, words with letters missing, and ungrammatical phrases and sentences that they use.

character's name	elided words	ungrammatical phrases and sentences	missing letters
Colin	you're	them's my clothes	probly

3 Using the evidence from question 2, decide which characters speak informally and which speak formally. You could grade them on a scale of 1-5. 1 is very informal and 5 is very formal.

Now count how many Australian slang words each character uses.

Keep a tally chart to get a final number.

Who uses the most slang?

Who uses the least slang?

Is it possible for a character to speak informally without using lots of slang?

Write a short paragraph on what you have discovered. Support your answer with evidence from the playscript.

4 Now go back to the opening dialogue. Try to re-write Colin's words in more formal English. How will you deal with Colin's joke about the kitchen sink?

What do you think of your finished version?

Which version do you prefer and why?

Comprehension

1 Who will Colin stay with in England? List the names of all the members of the family.

2 List the three reasons Colin's mum gives to persuade Colin that he will have a great time staying with his relatives in London.

3 Who does Colin tell the captain he is going see when he gets to London? What reason does he give for this? Answer in sentences.

4 How many times does Colin use the word 'cancer' in this extract?

5 What does he think are worse topics than cancer?

6 Why do you think the businessman asks the air hostess if there are any other seats available? What does Colin think he means?

7

a) Imagine that you ask each character in this passage what they think of Colin. Write down a sentence for each person giving their honest response to your question.

b) If Colin was in your class, what would be your opinion of him? Write a sentence which best sums it up.

8

a) Re-read the exclamation 'Bull!' and the first sentence of Colin's speech (line 27). What is Colin's very first reaction to the news about Luke?

b) Then re-read from 'They're bein' slack!' (line 27) to 'Bloody slack.' (line 34). Summarize Colin's thoughts in this section, in one sentence.
How does he feel about going to London? Look at the stage direction on line 29.

c) Next re-read from 'If it was somebody important' (line 34) to '... beside her in London.' (line 38). Summarize Colin's thoughts in this section in a sentence.

d) Finally, re-read from 'London!' (line 38) to the end of the speech. How does Colin now feel about going to London? Why has he changed his mind?

9

In Text A, Colin tries to talk to several adults about Luke's cancer. These are just some of the responses he gets.

A
Don't talk about things you don't understand.

B
Ar, em, yes, well...

C
Now when you write to Luke, don't say anything about... You know.

D
I know what it is. I just don't particularly want to talk about it.

E
Because it's not a very pleasant topic.

F
Don't talk about it. Please don't.

Mum   Dad   Businessman   Captain

Link the right adult with the right speech or speeches.
Why does each adult react in that way?

Write a sentence about each.

In this extract from *Two Weeks with the Queen*, what message is the author trying to put across about whether cancer should be discussed with children? Answer in a couple of sentences.

 10 Morris Gleitzman's novel *Two Weeks with the Queen* has been described as 'a remarkable, exciting, moving and funny book'.

a) Which were the funniest bits of the extract and why?

b) Did you find any parts of the script painful or sad? Describe which bits and give your reasons why.

c) Draw a scale like the one below. Mark on the scale where you place this extract.

very sad -- very funny
1   2   3   4   5   6   7   8   9   10

Compare your scale with other members of the class. Where do the majority of the marks fall?

Speaking and listening

1 **Pairs**

Note: the work you did on Comprehension question 8 will help you with this activity.

Look closely at Colin's speech below. For the purpose of this activity, it has been split into three parts.

Colin   Bull! I don't believe you! They're bein' slack! If they can sew a bloke's foot on and put a new heart in somebody surely they can cure a bit of cancer! [*He starts to throw his clothes angrily out of the suitcase.*] What about the man in the newsagents? He had cancer on his head and they cured him. Expect me to believe you can get the cricket from India and get bombs that could blow the whole world up and robots and space ships and they can't cure a bit of cancer! Bull! They're just not tryin'!

[*He slumps down.*] Bloody slack. If it was someone important they'd pull their finger out alright. If it was the Prime Minister they'd be askin' the Queen of England for the world's best doctor's phone number then, eh? I bet the Queen has the world's best doctor right there beside her in London.

London! [*He starts throwing the clothes back in the suitcase. He picks it up and leaves the room.*] Hey Mum. What time's my plane?

Work in pairs. Imagine you are directing this play. The actor playing Colin is struggling with this speech and you need to help him. You want 'Colin' to change his mood three times during this speech and this must be clear to the audience.

Together, decide on Colin's mood for each of the three sections. Then, working on a section at a time, jot down some suggestions to help the actor communicate Colin's feelings to the audience. You need to think about:

- his tone of voice
- the words he might emphasize
- his facial expressions
- his movements and body language.

Now try it out. You could work from your own suggestions or swap with another pair.

One of you should play the actor (Colin) and the other, the director. The director is allowed to stop the action and make suggestions to the actor whenever he/she thinks it is necessary. Remember: negative criticism will not produce the best results.
Try the speech several times and then swap roles.
Share your work with others in the class.
Which pairs have been the most successful in communicating Colin's change of moods to the audience?

2 **Whole class**

Organize and stage a class debate on the following question:

> Should children be protected from the 'painful truth' of life-threatening illness and death or do they have the right always to be kept informed?

You will need two small groups: one to support the right of the child to be kept informed and the other to argue that the decision what to tell a child must be the responsibility of the adults involved.

Each group then prepares its side of the argument.

Choose a spokesperson from each group.

In turn, both sides put forward their argument.

Allow time for audience questions and comments.

Then take a vote: **do** children have the right to be kept fully informed about life-threatening illness and death?

This debate will give you ideas for an essay on this subject (Writing Assignment 2).

TEXT B

The next poem was written by the Irish poet Seamus Heaney. He was born in 1939 in County Derry, Northern Ireland, and is considered to be one of Ireland's greatest poets. He has published several volumes of poetry and in 1995, he won the Nobel Prize for Literature. His poems are popular and appeal to a wide range of readers. He is inspired by his interest in history and the landscape, and mixes images from both in poems about his childhood, his family and friends, and the political and social situation in Northern Ireland.

Mid-term Break

I sat all morning in the college sick bay
Counting bells knelling classes to a close.
At two o'clock our neighbours drove me home.

In the porch I met my father crying –
He had always taken funerals in his stride –
And Big Jim Evans saying it was a hard blow.

The baby cooed and laughed and rocked the pram
When I came in, and I was embarrassed
By old men standing up to shake my hand

And tell me they were 'sorry for my trouble';
Whispers informed strangers I was the eldest,
Away at school, as my mother held my hand

In hers and coughed out angry tearless sighs.
At ten o'clock the ambulance arrived
With the corpse, stanched and bandaged by the nurses.

Next morning I went up into the room. Snowdrops
And candles soothed the bedside; I saw him
For the first time in six weeks. Paler now,

Wearing a poppy bruise on his left temple,
He lay in the four foot box as in his cot.
No gaudy scars, the bumper knocked him clear.

A four foot box, a foot for every year.

Seamus Heaney

WORD BANK

gaudy very brightly coloured

knelling the sound of a bell; usually used to describe bells rung to announce a death

sick bay an area of a boarding school where sick children stay

stanched or staunched; stopped the flow of blood

Comparison

1 Listen to your teacher read the poem aloud. What is your immediate reaction on reaching the end? Spend 60 seconds only, writing down words to describe the poem and your reaction to it. Keep this safe, you may need it later.

2 Read the poem yourself a stanza at a time and answer the following questions.

Stanza 1: What clues are there that something is wrong?

Stanza 2: Pick out the words and phrases that suggest that someone might be dead.

Stanzas 3 and 4: We are not yet told who is dead, but instead who is alive. Name the members of the narrator's family who we know are alive.

What evidence is there to make the reader think the victim is someone close to the narrator?

Stanza 5: Why do you think the poet uses the word 'corpse' and not the name of the dead person?

Stanza 6: What effect does the word 'soothed' create?

Stanza 7: What is the first clue that the dead person is a child?

Last line: What is the effect of the final line? Look at the choice of words and the way they are presented in relation to the rest of the poem.

3 Read the words you wrote as your immediate reaction to the poem. Having looked at the poem more closely, do you still feel the same way? If your feelings have changed, describe them and say why.

4 Pick out the line(s) from the poem which affected you most. Explain why you chose them and what they mean to you. Write a sentence for every line you have chosen.

5 'This poem is too sad to read with school children.' Write a short paragraph to explain why you agree or disagree with this statement.

6 Which text do you think is the most effective/did you like best – A or B? Explain why. You may want to comment on:

▶ the impact of the passage – how it made you feel and how long that feeling lasted
▶ the style – the difference between a playscript and a poem
▶ the characterization – how convincing the characters were
▶ the way it dealt with the subject of terminal illness /death.

Writing assignments

1 Write a follow-on scene for *Two Weeks with the Queen* to show what happens when Colin meets his English relations. Colin has a plan to save his brother and he is determined to contact the Queen to get her help. How will his aunt, uncle and cousin react to this? Will they support him or is he on his own?

You need to:

▶ decide how funny your scene will be and whether you will go for verbal or visual humour – or both
▶ remember to continue Colin's informal language and slang
▶ decide what sort of people Auntie Iris, Uncle Bob and Alistair are. The following information may give you some clues:

> **Uncle Bob** hates the royal family but loves DIY.
> **Auntie Iris** fusses over Alastair and nags him constantly about germs, standing up straight, picking scabs, brushing his teeth, etc.
> **Cousin Alistair** isn't allowed out on his own; too much excitement brings on his dandruff.

▶ think about their reaction to Luke's cancer. Will they discuss it openly or will they try to avoid the subject altogether?

2 In this unit, there are two passages which deal with the subjects of terminal illness and death. In *Two Weeks with the Queen*, Colin is sent away from the scene of illness (which might be fatal) and in *Mid-term Break*, the narrator is brought home after a death.

Write a discursive essay on the question:

Do children have the right to be kept fully informed about life-threatening illness and death?

You may find the following structure helpful to plan and write your essay.

Paragraph 1: introduction
Paragraph 2: one point of view (usually the one you disagree with)
Paragraph 3: the other point of view (usually the one you agree with)
Paragraph 4: a clear statement of your view leading to a conclusion.

The following phrases are useful for this kind of essay, in which you need to put two sides of an argument:

Paragraph 2	Paragraph 3
Some people feel that...	But other people argue
On the one hand...	However, on the other hand...

3 Using Heaney's *Mid-term Break* as your starting point, write a report for the local newspaper on the accident which kills the narrator's brother. This should be no more than 150 words long and should include facts from the poem. Start by making a list of these facts under the following headings.

▷ Details of the accident   ▷ Details about the victim's family
▷ Details about the victim   ▷ Any other relevant information

Now see where the gaps occur. Make up appropriate information to fill these gaps.

Don't forget to
▷ write a headline
▷ follow the 'golden rule' of journalism and answer the five Ws, preferably in your first paragraph:
<u>W</u>ho was involved? <u>W</u>hat happened? <u>W</u>hen? <u>W</u>here? <u>W</u>hy?

1 Fiction

And then...

In this unit you will:

- compare a fiction extract with a piece of autobiography – both about animals
- explore the way writers use discourse markers to structure stories
- put together a *Crimewatch* programme
- practise writing stories, autobiography, or an article for a magazine.

Language focus

How do you know when a story is a story? Look at these two extracts. One is a story; one is informative writing from a cereal packet. You will be able to tell the difference immediately – but how?

A
The child walked through the forest for a while and <u>then</u> felt tired. She paused <u>before</u> setting off <u>again</u> on her journey.

B
The key to looking and feeling good is a sensible balance of diet and exercise, and a healthy breakfast <u>therefore</u> has a valuable role to play.

Which are the key words which tell you that one text is a story? Which are the key words which tell you that the other text is an information text?

> **Discourse markers**
> Most texts use grammatical features called discourse markers. These are words and phrases that help the reader to follow the way a text is developing.

In a narrative or story text you might expect discourse markers like these:

Then
Later
Because
Meanwhile
Whilst

Discourse markers are useful because they signal to the reader

▶ how time is passing
▶ how one event in a story leads to the next, and the next.

TEXT A

Rachel Anderson was born in 1943. She has won various prizes for her children's stories. She lives in north Norfolk and likes growing strawberries. Her best-known fiction titles are *Princess Jazz and the Angels*, and *Letters from Heaven*. She also wrote *For the Love of Sang*, which describes how she and her family adopted a Vietnamese orphan with severe physical and learning difficulties.

Look at this extract from a short story by Rachel Anderson. It is about a boy called Matt who sneaks out of his house in the middle of the night to watch a total eclipse that his teacher has told him about. He is sitting in the edge of a wood waiting to see the eclipse...

Black and White

He wrapped the blanket round him and settled in the hedge. Kept as still as he could. That way, he felt he was less visible to whatever might be out there, watching. He tried not to listen to his heart pumping, his breathing coming and going in noisy gasps.

He kept looking at the moon.

Sir might have been right about the absence of light pollution. But there was more than enough very peculiar sound pollution. Trees sighing, branches creaking. Small dry scrabblings down in the grass. A snort from a horse. Then the worst one of all, the short but terrible shriek of a bird somewhere in the woods. It made Matt think of all those turkeys and whether they were still happy once they were dead.

He went on staring at the moon, waiting for the edges to begin disappearing. He thought it had started. But it was as round as ever. Still too early. He wished he had a watch.

He heard the dreadful shrieking in the woods again.

Then something began happening. But not what he expected. As he watched, he could hardly hold back his disappointment. How dare the weather do this? Those little soft clouds on the horizon were gathering together and moving nearer. They'd already blanketed half the sky and extinguished the stars. Now they were creeping towards the moon.

Matt stayed where he was and hoped. Sometimes weather changed quite fast. The sky might well clear again and he'd at least get to see the end of the eclipse.

The cloud-cover thickened. Nothing could glow through that lot. It had turned into an ordinary, cloudy night.

He was angry with the weather, with the darkness, with the moon for daring to promise so much and failing to deliver. It was stupid to have come out at all. He must go back in case Mum woke and wondered where he was.

He was just about to get to his feet when the creature appeared.

It came out between the trees and was moving steadily towards him, a huge white shape, as broad as an arm-span and flying level with his head. Silently, stealthily, with a ghostly pale face and dark staring eyes, it was following the line of the hedge. Matt thought it was going to crash right into him but he was too astonished to move.

But no. It came flying right up to him, looked him directly in the eye, and then lurched aside and went out over the meadow. Not a turkey's ghost, not a phantom rider, but an enormous owl.

Matt was no longer afraid. It had made eye contact and identified him as a fellow-creature of the night. He watched as it dipped along the course of the stream, then back, quartering the ground. And round again and again, lurching and searching. It must be hunting. Then, away out of sight into the woods.

So very white and so much larger than he'd have expected an owl to be. And it hadn't been afraid of him.

Where did it live? What did it do all day? And why did it shriek when owls were supposed to go tu-whit, tu-whoo?

Up till now, Matt realized, fear had been obscuring his vision of everything that was out here waiting to be seen. If he'd never come out, he'd never have known.

By morning, it was raining heavily. But Matt, walking up to the crossroads, kept his anorak hood back. Then he could watch the trees. I know you're in there somewhere, he thought.

That afternoon, everybody else in library time was scrabbling for the books on astronomy. Matt looked up birds.

Nests in old barns or big trees with suitable holes... Should be given every protection... Fast becoming rare in many areas... A variety of calls, the most common being a loud shriek... also makes hissing and snoring noises...

Yes, that was surely a barn owl he'd seen, going about its night-time business, and which had looked right at him. And that was what he wanted to write about.

After all, he hadn't, strictly speaking, seen anything of the eclipse so how could he write about it?

He went back to his desk. He opened his project book.

On second thoughts, maybe he'd keep the sighting of the barn owl to himself for a bit. Though he just might mention it to Mum.

He picked up his pen.

*Total Lunar Eclipses, he wrote and underlined it firmly.
An eclipse is any obscuring of light from one heavenly body by another.*

Rachel Anderson

Language questions

1 Here are some of the discourse markers the writer uses to organize her story. Use them to help you produce a flow chart which shows the structure of the story. The first part is done to get you started:

Discourse marker	What happened at this stage:
	Matt sat in the hedge
	⬇
Then	Clouds began to cover the moon
	⬇
He was just about to... when	⬇
Then	⬇
Up till now	⬇
By morning	⬇
That afternoon	⬇
On second thoughts	

2 Now try retelling the story in just three sentences using these discourse markers:

Once...
Later...
Finally...

Comprehension

1 What clues are there in the first paragraph that Matt feels nervous? See if you can find two.

2 How does the writer make the appearance of the owl seem mysterious?

3 Once he realizes it is an owl, why is Matt no longer afraid?

4 Early in the story Matt is disappointed not to see the eclipse. How can you tell later in the story that he has changed his mind?

5 Based on the extract, what picture do you get of Matt's character? Draw a spider diagram showing what you have learnt about him. Aim to make six points about him.

6 Matt decides not to write about the barn owl at school. Instead he writes about the eclipse, even though he did not see it. In your own words say why you think he does this.

7 Rachel Anderson calls her story *Black and White*. Try to write a sentence explaining what the title might mean.

Speaking and listening

1 **Pairs**

Imagine Matt returns home in the early hours of the morning after seeing the barn owl. His mum doesn't know he's been out. He wants to keep his adventure a secret. But when he closes the door, his mum hears him and comes downstairs to find out what is going on.

Improvise the conversation that takes place. Before you begin:

If you are playing Matt, decide what he will do. Will he tell his mum where he's been? Will he tell her about the owl?

If you are playing Mum, decide how you will react to Matt's sudden appearance, fully dressed and apparently just returning home in the middle of the night. Will you be angry, worried, curious?

The role play might begin like this:

Mum	Who's that? Who's down there?
Matt	Mum, it's me, Matt.
Mum	Matthew! What are you doing up at this hour of the night? And why are you dressed in your outdoor clothes...?

2 Groups

Pick out one of your group to be Matt. The rest of the group is going to interview him on the events of the night, which have made a powerful impression on him.

If you are playing Matt, re-read the story, concentrating on how Matt feels about what has happened.

If you are in the interviewing group, compile a list of questions you would like to ask him – about
- what he was doing
- what he saw
- how he felt at the time
- how he feels now
- why he feels this way.

When you are ready, put Matt 'in the hot seat'.

TEXT B

The next text is all about a different creature – a monkey. It is written by the well-known nature writer, Gerald Durrell.

Gerald Durrell was born in 1925, and has been fascinated by animals since he was a child. His most famous book is probably *My Family and Other Animals*, which describes his childhood with his extraordinary family and their pets. He grew up to become a writer and zoologist.

This extract is set in Cameroon, a country in West Africa. Gerald is sharing his quarters with a variety of animals, including forty monkeys; some of them are injured wild animals which have been brought to him for treatment. A young woman visitor has been lecturing him on how cruel it is to keep animals in the way he does – surely the monkeys would be happier living in the wild. He decides to put her to the test...

A Wilderness of Monkeys

THAT MORNING A BABY MONKEY had been brought in by a native hunter, and since the young lady seemed to be such an expert on monkey life in the tree-tops, I suggested that she might like to help me perform a little task that had to be gone through with each monkey that arrived. She agreed eagerly, seeing herself in the role of a sort of simian Florence Nightingale.

The little task consisted, quite simply, in searching the new baby for internal and external parasites. I explained this, and the young lady looked surprised: she said that she did not know that monkeys had parasites – beyond fleas, of course. I produced the little basket that the monkey was brought in, and removing some of its excreta I spread it out on a clean piece of paper and showed her the numbers of threadlike worms it contained. My helper remained strangely silent. Then I brought out the baby: he was a Putty-nose Guenon, an adorable little fellow clad in black fur, with a white shirtfront and a gleaming, heart-shaped patch of white fur on his nose. I examined his tiny hands and feet and his long slender fingers and toes and found no fewer than six jiggers comfortably ensconced. These minute creatures burrow their way into the skin of the feet and hands, particularly under the nails, where the skin is soft, and there they eat and swell and grow, until they reach the size of a match-head. Then they lay their eggs and die; in due course the eggs hatch and the baby jiggers continue the good work that their parent had begun. If a jigger infection is not dealt with in the early stages it can lead to the loss of the joint of a toe or finger, and in extreme cases it can destroy all the toes and fingers, for the jiggers go on burrowing and breeding until they have hollowed the part out to a bag of skin filled with pus. I have had jiggers in my foot on several occasions, and can vouch for the fact that they can be extremely painful. All this I explained to my helper in graphic detail. Then I got the tube of local anaesthetic, froze the fingers and toes of the little Guenon, and with a sterilized needle proceeded to remove the jiggers and disinfect the wounds they left. I found this local anaesthetic a boon, for the operation is painful and the baby monkeys would not sit still otherwise.

When this was over I ran my fingers down the monkey's tail and felt two sausage-shaped swellings, each as long as the first joint of my little finger and about the same circumference. I showed these to my companion, and then parted the hair so that she could see the circular, porthole-like opening at the end of each swelling. Looking through this porthole into the interior of the swelling, you could see something white and loathsome moving. I explained, with my best Harley Street air, that a certain forest fly lays its eggs on the fur of various animals, and when the maggot hatches it burrows down into the flesh of its host and lives there, fattening like a pig in a sty, getting air through the porthole, and, when it finally leaves to turn into a fly, the host has a hole the circumference of a cigarette in its flesh, which generally becomes a suppurating sore. I showed my helper, who was by now quite pale, that it was impossible to hook these maggots out. I got the needle and, parting the hair, showed her the creature lying in its burrow like a miniature barrage balloon; as soon as the tip of the needle touched it, however, it just compressed itself into a wrinkled blob, folding up like a concertina, and slid back into the depths of the monkey's tail. Then I showed her how to get them out – a method I had invented: pushing the nozzle of the anaesthetic tube into the porthole, I squirted the liquid inside until I had frozen the maggot into immobility; then, with a scalpel, I enlarged the porthole slightly, stabbed the maggot with the end of the needle and withdrew it from its lair. As I pulled the wrinkled white horror out of the bloodstained hole, my helper left me suddenly and precipitately. I removed the second maggot, disinfected the gaping holes they had left and then joined her at the other side of the camp clearing. She explained that she was late for a lunch date, thanked me for a most interesting morning, and took her leave, never to visit us again. I always think it rather a pity that people don't learn more about the drawbacks of life in the jungle before prating about the cruelty of captivity.

Gerald Durrell

WORD BANK

ensconced hidden away
Florence Nightingale a famous nurse of the 19th century
Harley Street London street famous for its medical practitioners

prating babbling
precipitately before we had finished
simian relating to monkeys
suppurating oozing

Comparison

1 What sort of monkey is Gerald Durrell treating in this extract?

2 How many different types of parasite does he find on the monkey? List them.

3 Why is it impossible at first to hook the maggots out of the monkey's tail?

4 Although this is a non-fiction text, Gerald Durrell uses some of the same discourse markers that you have already found in the Rachel Anderson story. He has to use discourse markers to show the process he went through ('I did this... then I did this') after the monkey was brought to him. Look through the story and list the discourse markers you can find. (Sometimes he uses the same one several times over.)

5 Gerald Durrell also puts two blocks of information into this extract, when he describes
a) the lifecycle of a parasite called a 'jigger'
b) the lifecycle of the forest fly which lays its eggs in the monkey's fur.

Choose one of these examples and write out the information, this time as a list of numbered points. When you have finished, underline any discourse markers you have used.
You might begin like this:

(1) Jiggers burrow their way into the skin of feet or hands.
(2) Then they begin to eat the flesh...

Or

(1) A forest fly lays its eggs in an animal's fur.
(2) When the eggs hatch...

6 When Gerald Durrell starts to describe the lifecycle of a jigger ('These minute creatures burrow...'), the style of the text changes. When he finishes the description and goes back to his narrative ('All this I explained...') the style changes again. See if you can describe in a sentence what the change is.

Hint Look at the tenses, and also look at Gerald Durrell's use of the word 'I'.

7 What do you think Gerald Durrell feels about the parasites he finds on the monkeys? Explain in a sentence, picking out words from the text to support your answer.

Hint Look in particular at the adjectives.

8 The operation to remove the parasites from the baby monkey sounds revolting.
a) What does Gerald Durrell's description of it make you feel about him?
b) Do you think he was fair to make the young woman watch it?

Writing assignments

1 Write up the scene when Matt returns to his house in the early hours. If you improvised the scene between Matt and his mum in Speaking and Listening activity 1, you could base your writing on that. Remember: Matt has just returned home, only to be met by his mum, who wants to know where he's been...

Write it as a scene in the novel, using dialogue to show what was said, and description to help the reader visualize the scene. You might begin:

The house was quiet as Matt pulled the door closed behind him...

You might want to use discourse markers like these to structure the scene:

Then	After a while
Later	Although

2 Gerald Durrell writes about his memories of living with animals. Think of a pet you have known, and choose one incident you particularly remember. It might be:
- getting the pet for the first time
- your hamster escaping from its cage
- your cat getting injured in a fight
- your dog having to go to the vet.

In your account, aim to:
- describe the animal in as much detail as possible
- describe what happened so that the reader can see the scene in his or her mind.

3 Some people think keeping pets is a good thing. It gives humans something to look after, can make them feel less lonely, and the animals enjoy having a loving owner.

Other people might think keeping pets is cruel and unnecessary. We tame animals and spoil their chances of ever living a natural life in the wild. We make them depend on us for food. We make them live in environments that do not suit them.

What do you think?

Are there some animals which should not be kept as pets?

Are there some animals which benefit from being kept as pets?

Write a 200-word article for a school magazine giving your opinion of the pros and cons of keeping pets. Start by making notes under two headings:

For keeping animals as pets	Against keeping animals as pets

When you write up your article:

▷ make your style direct and lively, using phrases like:

Keeping pets is...
I strongly disagree with those who say that...
Humans should...

▷ use questions to get your reader involved, e.g.:

Is keeping pets fair? Or is it cruel and inhumane?

▷ use discourse markers like these to signal the direction of your argument:

Another reason...
On the other hand...
Although...
But...
It is also the case...

Fiction

Looking at legends

2

Aims

In this unit you will:
- learn exactly what a legend is
- explore the way legends are usually written in formal written language – and how they sound when they are not
- explore other style features of legends
- discuss legends from your local area
- practise writing a legend of your own.

Language focus

Stories are written in a range of different styles.

Some are written in a simple style. This is especially true of stories with a lot of action in them, or stories which are written for children, e.g.

> Snap was a small black and white dog. He was the boss dog of Blossom Street.
>
> Rita Ray, *The Boss Dog of Blossom Street*

Some are told in a complex style – especially if they are written for older readers, or include a lot of description, or were written many years ago:

> He did not want the warm clover and the play of seeding grasses; the screens of quickset, billowy drapery seemed best away; and with great cheerfulness of spirit he pushed on towards the Wild Wood, which lay before him low and threatening, like a black reef in some still southern sea.
>
> Kenneth Grahame, *The Wind in the Willows*

Some are told in a chatty style – which is very close to the style of spoken language:

> Poor old Robin Hood, he led a wretched life...
> Little John and Friar Tuck ate all the grub.
> Maid Marian gave him a hard time.
>
> Dick King-Smith, *Robin Hood and his Miserable Men*

Other stories are told in a formal style, and we will be looking at an example of this in this unit.

Formal language

Formal language does not have to be complex. It can be very simple. But it will include certain features:

- Most or all of the sentences will be 'grammatically correct' – that is, they will all have a subject and a main verb.

- The author will avoid using slang words like 'grub' and informal phrases like 'gave him a hard time'; instead a formal story would use 'food' and 'complained ceaselessly to him'.

In this unit we'll be looking in particular at legends. Legends often use a formal style of written language, with words and phrases that we would not usually expect in less formal texts.

TEXT A

Now read this short written legend and explore the features of the style. It is taken from a book about walking written by Mike Harding.

Mike Harding was born in Lancashire in 1944. He is well known as a comedian and singer, but also has a passion for walking in the Yorkshire Dales. He is a keen photographer and a past president of the Ramblers' Association.

During one of his walks in the Yorkshire Dales he comes across a lake called Semer Water and pauses to describe a local legend...

Walking the Dales

WORD BANK

raiment gown

Like many lakes, Semer Water has its legendary sunken village or town, complete with underwater church bells tolling as storm winds move the surface of the lake. The story of the sunken village under Semer Water has been repeated so many times that it may be pointless me telling the story once again, yet there may be some of you who won't have heard it, so if you're sitting comfortably, I'll begin.

Once upon a time, an angel came down to earth to test the charity of man. Where Semer Water stands now there stood a fine city with towers, domes and spires reaching to the sky, and its streets, houses and shops were full of busy people. The angel, disguised as an old man, went from door to door begging for food and drink. At all of them he was turned away empty-handed and was cursed at as a beggar by the proud townspeople of Semer Water. On his way out of the city he came to a poor crofter's cottage. He knocked on the door and begged for aid. The old couple, poor as they were, took pity on him and gave him food to eat and water to drink. Then, throwing off his tattered rags and appearing in 'bright, shining raiment', the angel raised his staff and cried:

Semer Water rise, Semer Water sink,
And swallow all save this lile [little] house
That gave me meat and drink.

At the far end of Semer Water is a ruined building that is said to be the dwelling place of the charitable old couple. On summer evenings rowers on the lake have claimed that they have heard far below them through the still waters the sound of church bells tolling. There may be a basis of fact in the legend of Semer Water in that the lake is known to be the site of an Iron Age lake village built on piles out from the shore. ◑

Mike Harding

Language questions

1   Here are two ingredients of a formal style which are often used in written legends. For each one, see if you can find an example from the Semer Water legend:
a) a word or phrase which suggests we are reading a story
b) a serious rather than comic tone.

2   Written legends can also include:
a) 'types' of characters rather than specific names (e.g. <u>a girl</u> rather than <u>Sarah</u>)
b) complex rather than simple vocabulary (<u>enchanted</u> rather than <u>strange</u>)
Look again at the Semer Water legend and see if you can find an example of each of these.

3   Look at the following chart. On the left hand side are formal words and phrases – all found in the Semer Water legend. For each entry, see if you can write an informal word or phrase – for instance, the sort of word you might use if you were telling the story aloud to a friend. You may have to find different vocabulary, but sometimes you will also have to change the order of the words. One has been done for you:

Formal word or phrase	Informal word or phrase
to test the charity of man	
At all of them he was turned away	
begged for aid	
poor as they were	although they were poor
dwelling place	

4 Now try the same process in reverse. Look at these phrases. Try to find a more formal phrase you could use instead:

Informal word or phrase	Formal word or phrase
He was feeling down in the dumps.	
'Not on your life!' I yelled.	
He thumped the guard and legged it.	
He was grinning from ear to ear.	

5 Have a go at writing the first four sentences of the Semer Water legend in an informal style.

Comprehension

1 At the beginning of the second paragraph, which word tells us that we are about to read a story rather than fact?

2 In your own words, say why the angel comes down to earth.

3 The writer describes the townspeople of Semer Water as 'proud'. What does the word mean in this context?

4 What impression do we get of what the city was like? Write a sentence to describe it.

5 The old couple lived in a crofter's cottage. Why do you think it was on the edge of the city?

6 This text is a mixture of storytelling and opinion. Part of it tells us the legend of Semer Water. Part of it tells us about the lake today. Look at the last sentence of the extract. How can you tell that this is **not** telling a story?

7 Which of these statements best sums up Mike Harding's view of the legend? Write a sentence saying how you can tell:

- He thinks the tale is probably true.
- He thinks the tale is definitely true.
- He doesn't give a personal opinion.
- He thinks the tale is probably false.
- He thinks the tale is definitely false.

8 Legends are always a mixture of fact and fiction. Finish these two sentences:

a) There is some evidence that the Semer Water legend may be true because...

b) There is some evidence that it may be untrue because...

Speaking and listening

1 **Pairs**

In pairs, develop a TV interview between a journalist and someone who has managed to escape the sudden flooding which has drowned the city at Semer Water.

If you are playing the news reporter, talk to camera about what has happened and then interview the eyewitness about what he or she has seen. Ask open rather than closed questions. For example:

> Open question: What did you see today?
> Closed question: Did you see the flooding today?

If you are playing the survivor, try to imagine what an eyewitness account of the flooding of Semer Water would be like. How do you feel now? Do you feel the proud people of Semer Water deserved to perish for turning the beggar away? Or are you distressed and enraged by what has happened?

TEXT B

Tony Robinson and Richard Curtis are well known for their comic writing. Tony Robinson played Baldrick in the series *Blackadder*, as well as many other television roles. He was author of the children's series *Maid Marian*, and *Blood and Honey*, a retelling of some Bible stories. Richard Curtis wrote most of the *Blackadder* series, as well as the screenplays of *Four Weddings and a Funeral* and *Notting Hill*.

In this extract, the Greek hero Theseus, Prince of Athens, is about to be fed to a terrible bull-like monster, the Minotaur, which lives in a maze of caves on the island of Crete and feeds on human flesh. The maze is so deep that once inside, Theseus may never find his way out again. He has been warned to take a ball of string with him, to mark his way through the caves – but he and his friends still have to face the Minotaur. The only things strong enough to pierce its hide are the horns on its own head...

Theseus, Monster-Killer

At noon the cell doors swung open and the Athenians began their journey to the maze. They marched for miles down gloomy winding corridors. Cold and damp began to seep into their bodies as they plunged deeper and deeper into the bowels of the earth. The walls were rougher than the stubble on a giant's beard and tiny, slithery animals jumped on them and nipped at them as they passed, having a nibble before the Minotaur had his big meal. Then, at the end of a long flight of slippery steps covered with green slime, they saw ahead of them a gigantic carved bull's head with blazing torches for eyes, and a massive black studded door where its mouth should have been. The Minoan guards heaved the door open and the Athenians were roughly shoved inside. There was a slam, then a rattle of chains and the door was bolted behind them.

They were inside the maze. And if history was anything to go by, it was the door of their coffin that had just closed behind them.

It was pitch black, and they had to grope about to get their bearings.

'AAAARRGHHH!!!' Someone let out a terrified scream: he'd tripped over something. It was a skull – a human skull. One of the young men began to moan with terror.

'Oh, get a grip!' snapped Theseus sharply. 'Here. Do something useful. Tie this string to the door. I'm going exploring.' And with that, he began to inch his way through the maze, unrolling the ball of string as he went. The other Athenians just assumed he'd gone mad and waited for their death.

The walls were jagged and sharp, like enormous stone thorns; they tore at Theseus' clothes and ripped his hands. And now he could smell the foul stench he had noticed when they first arrived – a smell of sewage, and rotting meat and death – it was so strong his stomach churned and his eyes watered.

GRRIAAAOOW!!

He started in fright as the blood-thirsty bull's roar resounded in his ears and echoed and re-echoed round every wall of the maze.

Then there was silence. Everything was quiet and still.

First Theseus waited. Then cautiously he turned a sharp corner. Ahead of him was something dark and enormous with blazing yellow eyes and hot breath. In the half light its shiny skin glistened like the skin of a toad – but it was twice the size of an elephant.

Theseus knew he was face to face with death itself.

But there was no time to be afraid – in a second there was a clatter of enormous hooves and the beast reared and charged at Theseus, slobbering and chuckling as it came. Theseus leapt and dodged out of its way. A moment's silence, then a crunch of stones as the monstrous bull turned and charged again. Again Theseus dodged, and this time the Minotaur's horns missed him by a cat's whisker – and a pretty skinny whisker at that. There was a screech of pebbles, and it charged yet again. Theseus made to jump, but instead, his foot slipped on something disgusting and wet. It might

have been a kidney. The Prince of Athens fell defenceless on the floor.

The Minotaur seemed to know it had won. It let out a triumphant bellow and lowered its head to deliver the final thrust. But when it was almost on him, Theseus sprang up with a last burst of energy and vaulted astride the monster's head, riding it like a wild bull. He grasped one of its horns, and heaved and twisted. There was a terrible crunching sound, like a young tree being torn out of the earth by its roots.

Then…

Back at the entrance, the Athenians heard a terrible cry. A death cry. They waited in terror. Then they heard the sound of something coming towards them. It was

breathing heavily. They clung to each other, knowing death was on its way. And then…

'Wow – I'm puffed!' said Theseus. 'Anyone want a ball of string?'

The Athenians were so stunned with relief, they couldn't speak.

'Oh, yes, and by the way – the Minotaur's dead,' added the young hero.

Tony Robinson and *Richard Curtis*

Comparison

1 Pick out two details which show the tunnels and caves are unpleasant to be in.

2 Look again at the first part of the story, up to where Theseus sees the Minotaur. What impression do you get of Theseus' character? Write down two of your own words to describe what he is like.

3 What is the Minotaur like? Based on the details given in the extract, draw a quick sketch of the creature, labelling it with details given in the passage.

4 The writers use a number of techniques to entertain the reader with their retelling of this legend. Try to find an example of each of the following:

a) characters' dialogue which uses a chatty style

b) comic words or descriptions

c) informal rather than formal words and phrases.

5 To help us picture the scene, the writers use comparisons – for example, comparing the Minotaur's skin to that of a toad. Find two other examples of comparisons they use.

6 Mike Harding's retelling of the Semer Water legend used formal written language. This legend is much more informal. Look at these opinions and see which one you most agree with. Then write a sentence explaining why:

a) Text B is funnier but doesn't feel as much like a legend as Text A.

b) Text A is too formal. Text B is more entertaining.

c) Text B trivializes the legend – it entertains us but we don't really feel involved in the story.

d) Text B makes the story feel more up-to-date and easier to follow.

7 Now write a brief paragraph saying whether you prefer the style of Text A or the style of Text B, and why. Try to be as precise as you can.

Writing assignments

1 Using Mike Harding's story about Semer Water, rewrite it as a legend for children. Aim to make it as eerie and fascinating as possible, getting the reader really involved.

Think about:

▶ how you will start the story – will you choose a different starting point from Mike Harding?

▶ what style you will use – a formal one like Mike Harding's or a more informal, conversational one like Tony Robinson and Richard Curtis's tale?

▶ Whether you will add more detail to the people in the story – for instance, will you describe the angel/beggar and the old couple in more detail? Will you give them names? Will you describe the old couple's house?

▶ how you will end the story – what can you do to make it really mysterious?

Here are two possible opening sentences you could use to get started:

A Many years ago there was a fine city of towers and churches, grand houses and wide streets. It was called...

B Look out across the water and you'd think it had always been like this. But stop. Look carefully – and listen. Hear those bells? See those reeds poking above the water? What if they weren't reeds? What if they were the very tips of some old church spires? Well listen to this...

2 Theseus has agreed to take part in an on-line interview about his heroic battle with the Minotaur. Members of his fan club have emailed questions to him. Look at the questions below and, based on the text in this unit, write down the answers he might give.

a) Were you at all nervous about meeting the Minotaur?

b) What was it like in those caves before you actually saw the creature?

c) What was going through your mind as you waited for the battle to begin?

d) What was the Minotaur really like?

e) How easy was it to kill the Minotaur?

f) How did your Athenian friends react when they saw you were safe?

g) If you were going into battle with the Minotaur again, what would you do differently?

Try to give some impression of Theseus' personality in your answers.

3 Choose a legend from your local area – about a lane or house that's haunted, an abandoned hospital where something awful happened, or someone who used to live nearby. Imagine you have been asked to retell the legend for parents of students at your school, in a special anniversary newsletter. Try to bring the legend to life in less than 400 words.

Or invent a legend about your school. Who built it? What was on the site before the school was started? What if it was a swamp, or a home to some legendary creature?

Create a legend that will make readers want to read on and find out more.

Fiction

Horror!

Aims

In this unit you will:
- ▶ look at the way writers tell horror stories
- ▶ examine how they build suspense
- ▶ discuss why people like horror stories so much
- ▶ write your own horror story.

Language focus

Horror stories deal with the subjects of our nightmares – rats, spiders, being buried alive, meeting creatures from beyond the grave. Since the earliest stories were told, human beings have loved listening to, reading and watching horror stories.

Shakespeare's most popular play in his time was *Titus Andronicus*. In it, two villains are mashed up into a pie, baked, and then served for dinner to their mother.

A good horror story keeps us guessing – it builds suspense, making us wonder in terror what might happen next.

Horror writing comes in a variety of styles, but there are some features which are common to almost all good horror stories.

Use of detail

Horror authors describe key details of any scene to make it seem real and believable to the reader. (If the reader isn't convinced by what's happening, he or she won't be scared – and what should be frightening will seem instead ridiculous.) Adding detail in moments of suspense also builds up the tension, by forcing the reader to wait to find out what happens next.

Authors can add detail through:
- ▶ **adjectives** – to tell us what things were like
- ▶ careful choice of **verbs** – to show us exactly how people moved or behaved.

Mix of long and short sentences

Authors will use longer sentences to build up a picture of what is happening – then suddenly drop in a short sentence, to pull the reader up sharply, e.g.:

He gathered up the books and headed for the classroom door. He did not know what made him pause halfway across the room and look back towards the window. And there it was: the hand.

Plot twists

What makes a horror story frightening? Usually it isn't the amount of blood and gore the author describes. Instead, it is an unexpected twist of the plot which scares us. The plot of *Titus Andronicus* is a good example of a plot with a 'sting in the tale': the two villains are not just killed; they are served to their mother in a pie. The texts you are about to read also spring unexpected surprises on the reader.

TEXT A

Philippa Pearce was born in a Cambridgeshire village where she now lives, having spent many years in London. She worked as a radio producer and book editor, before becoming a full-time writer. Her novel *Tom's Midnight Garden* won The Carnegie Medal in 1958 and is generally acknowledged as a modern classic.

Examine the way Philippa Pearce builds suspense and creates a feeling of horror using attention to detail, in this extract from a horror story.

Andy and his parents are staying in the house of his Great Aunt Enid after she has been taken into hospital. She has always avoided letting anyone into her house. Now Andy is spending a night there...

THE DOG GOT THEM

Andy woke up in what seemed the middle of the night, but the room was not really dark. He thought he had been woken by a noise: a squeaking, perhaps. Now he was almost sure there was a soft scrabbling sound from the floor beyond the bottom of the bed. Very quietly he raised himself on his

elbow to look. Against the far wall, heads together as if conferring, were two rats. They must be rats, and yet they were much, much larger than any ordinary rat, and their colour was a grey white splotched with chestnut brown. He disliked their colouring very much. They seemed to have heard the slight creak of Andy's bedsprings, for now they turned their heads to look at him. They had pink eyes.

Then they began creeping to and fro against the wall, and then running, in an agitated kind of way, almost as if they were getting their courage up. Each time they ran in the direction of the bed, they ran nearer than they had done the last time. Especially the bigger of the two rats, which Andy assumed to be the male. The female lagged behind a little, always; but still she ran a little nearer to the bed every time.

The male rat was scurrying closer and closer, and suddenly the knowledge came to Andy that it was going to attack. He was appalled. Frantically he prepared to ward off its attack with his naked hand. The rat sprang, launching its heavy body through the air like a missile, and sank its teeth into his hand.

Andy was already on his feet on the bed. He knew the female rat would attack next. The male hung from his hand as he slapped it violently, madly, repeatedly against the wall so that the body of the iron-teethed monster banged again and again and again against the wall. It seemed to him that almost simultaneously the body of the rat suddenly flew from its head, still teeth-clenched in his flesh, and he himself flew from the dreadful bedroom. He slammed the door behind him against the female rat, and rushed into his parents' room. They had already put on the light, roused by his screaming.

Andy was still screaming: 'Look! The rat – the rat!' He held out his hand for them to see the horror hanging from it.

They all looked at his hand: Andy's brown right hand, just as it always had been, entirely unmarked except where he had once scarred himself with a saw long ago. No rat.

WORD BANK

conferring holding a discussion
simultaneously at exactly the same time

'You've been dreaming,' said his mother. 'You were asleep and you had a nightmare.'

'No,' said Andy, 'I was awake.' And he told them everything.

They went back into the spare-room with him. There were no rats of course, nor any sign of one.

Philippa Pearce

Language questions

1 Look back at the first three sentences. The writer uses 'delaying' tactics here: hinting at something unpleasant without telling the reader what it is. Try to find three examples of specific words she uses to suggest that something odd is going on.

2 Look at the detail the writer uses to describe the rats. Write down three adjectives she uses to help us visualize what they look like.

3 Another way of creating detail is through careful choice of verbs. Instead of using a verb and adverb such as 'The man *walked slowly*', you could say 'the man *meandered / limped / shuffled* along'. These help us to visualize the scene more powerfully.

Look at the verbs listed below. For each one, think of a different verb and adverb the writer might have used instead:
a) Then they began *creeping* to and fro
b) The female *lagged* behind
c) The male rat was *scurrying*
d) The rat *sprang*

4 Pick out and write down two examples of a long sentence followed by a very short one. See if you can find one in paragraph 1, another in paragraph 3.

5 Write down in your own words what the 'twist' is at the end of this extract.

Comprehension

1 What do we learn about the rats during the extract? Fill in as many details as you can in a table like this:

number	
colour	
any other features	
unpleasant words used to describe them	
words used to describe the way they move	

2 In what way are these rats different from what Andy expects rats to be like?

3 What impression of the rats do you get from these descriptions:
a) 'heads together as if conferring'
b) 'launching its heavy body through the air like a missile'
c) 'the iron-teethed monster'?

Write a sentence about each description, on what it tells you about the rats.

4 What clues are there that Andy has been dreaming?

5 What impression do you get of Andy from the extract? Choose the three words from the following list which you think best describe him:

brave mad afraid startled confused angry
hallucinating determined

Then write a short paragraph explaining why you have chosen those words.

6 Write a paragraph predicting what happens next.

Are the rats just in Andy's imagination? Do they really exist? Does he see them again?

You might use phrases like this:

> In the next part of the story I predict that... .
> I think that...
> I expect...
> I imagine that...

(Keep your notes safe – you may want to refer to them if you do Writing Assignment 1.)

Speaking and listening

1 **Small group**

Imagine the news of a rat-infested house gets out. Journalists are fascinated by this story of a boy attacked by rats as he sleeps. Working in a small group of three or four, put together the news report that might be broadcast on the local radio station.

You should include:

▶ the newsreader who introduces the story
▶ the reporter at the scene (perhaps outside the house)
▶ some witnesses who comment – perhaps Andy and a neighbour.

Start by making some notes about what information each person is going to give. (Don't give all the facts at the beginning, or your listeners may switch off.) The following script outline will help you plan your role play:

VOICE	SCRIPT
Announcer	A boy was last night attacked by a large pack of rats as he slept in his Great Aunt's house.
	[Give more details.]

	Here from the scene is reporter, [give name].
Reporter	Neighbours have woken shocked and disturbed this morning as they learn about the events of last night …
	[Continue report.]
Andy/ neighbour	[Interviewed by reporter]
Reporter	[signing off] This is [name] reporting for [name of radio station].

2 Small group

Talk about why people are interested in horror stories. One of you should serve as chair of the discussion. Your role is:
- to keep the discussion moving
- to introduce new topics or questions when it begins to drag
- to make sure that everyone in the group voices an opinion.

Use the following discussion points to get you started:
- Think of horror stories and films you have read or seen. Why did you want to read or see them?
- What kind of horror did they use – phobias (things we are deeply frightened of), nightmares, death, violence?
- Why do you think people like horror films? Try to come up with four possible reasons.
- Do you think that horror stories can be harmful?

TEXT B

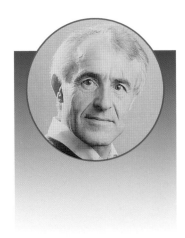

Creatures have often been a source of horror. People often have phobias about rats, spiders and other insects, but another source of horror stories has been creatures of legend, such as vampires, zombies and werewolves.

Look at the way use of detail creates a sense of horror in this poem by Jon Stallworthy. He is perhaps best known as an editor of poetry books - in particular, poetry of the First World War – but he is also an accomplished poet himself.

The Trap

The first night that the monster lurched
Out of the forest on all fours
He saw its shadow in his dream
Circle the house, as though it searched
For one it loved or hated. Claws
On gravel and a rabbit's scream
Ripped the fabric of his dream.

Waking between dark and dawn
And sodden sheets, his reason quelled
The shadow and the nightmare sound.
The second night it crossed the lawn
A brute voice in the darkness yelled.
He struggled up, woke raving, found
His wall-flowers trampled to the ground.

When rook wings beckoned the shadows back
He took his rifle down, and stood
All night against the leaded glass.
The moon ticked round. He saw the black
Elm-skeletons in the doomsday wood,
The sailing and the failing stars
And red coals dropping between bars.

WORD BANK

quelled calmed, forced to be quiet
putrid foul-smelling, like rotten meat
coverlet bed-covering, quilt
oppressed weighed down on
discerned saw
guillotined cut off (the guillotine was a machine for beheading people)
exultant triumphant

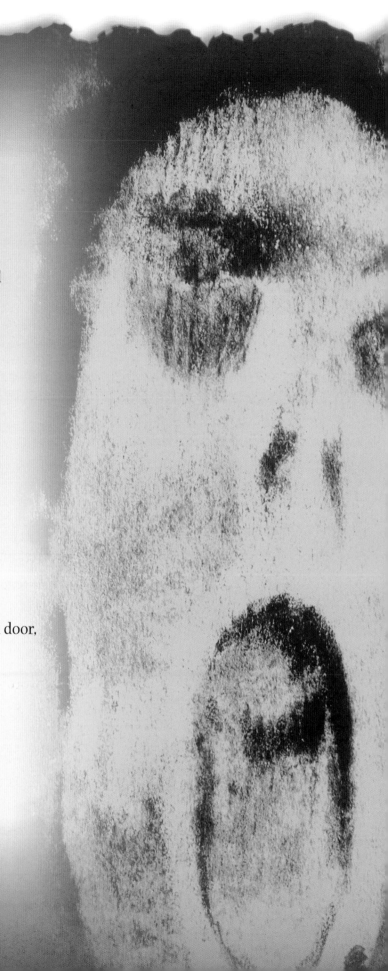

The third night such a putrid breath
Fouled, flared his nostrils, that he turned,
Turned, but could not lift, his head.
A coverlet as thick as death
Oppressed him: he crawled out: discerned
Across the door his watchdog, dead.
'Build a trap,' the neighbours said.

All that day he built his trap
With metal jaws and a spring as thick
As the neck of a man. One touch
Triggered the hanging teeth: jump, snap,
And lightning guillotined the stick
Thrust in its throat. With gun and torch
He set his engine in the porch.

The fourth night in their beds appalled
His neighbours heard the hunting roar
Mount, mount to an exultant shriek.
At daybreak timidly they called
His name, climbed through the splintered door,
And found him sprawling in the wreck,
Naked, with a severed neck.

Jon Stallworthy

Comparison

1 Start by jotting down a rough outline of the events described in the poem. Use this grid to help you. Some entries have been filled in for you.

Stanza	When it is set	What happens in it
1	The first night	
2	The next morning The second night	He wakes up and tries to forget the 'nightmare' He wakes and finds his flowers trampled
3		He keeps watch with his gun but sees nothing
4	The third night	
5	The next day	
6	The fourth night	

2 Use the prompts below to explore the poem stanza by stanza.

Stanza 1

a) Who do you think 'he' is?

b) The writer is deliberately holding back information about the monster. He only gives us a few details. What can we learn about it in this stanza? See if you can find three points.

Stanza 2

a) When he wakes up, the man thinks he must have had a bad dream. What word in line 3 tells you this?

b) After the second night, what clues does the man find that the monster is real?

Stanza 3

a) What do you think the writer might mean by 'the moon ticked round'?

b) Two other details in this stanza show time passing. Can you write down one of them?

c) Nothing appears that night, while the man keeps watch.

However, the writer uses two words to describe the wood which suggest something bad is going to happen. Write them down.

Stanza 4

a) In this stanza the man doesn't see the monster – he smells it. But he's unable to move. Write down the words that tell us this.

b) The man gets more evidence that the monster is real. What happens?

c) What do the man's neighbours tell him to do?

Stanza 5

a) Describe in your own words what the trap is like.

b) What do the words 'neck of a man', 'throat', and 'guillotined' suggest will happen next?

Stanza 6

What happens?

3 The last stanza gives the 'twist' at the end of the story – but what really happens? There are at least three explanations:

▶ The monster never existed – it was all in the man's mind.

▶ The monster was real – it lured him into the trap.

▶ The man was a werewolf but did not know it.

Write down how you think the man came to die. You need to find evidence from the poem to back up your theory.

4 Which text contains a stronger sense of horror – *The Dogs Got Them* or *The Trap*? Try to explain why.

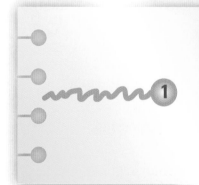

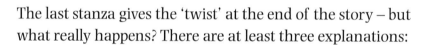

Writing assignments

1 Look back at Philippa Pearce's tale of the rats. What do you think happens next?

Write a continuation of the story. You might start with Andy searching the room with his parents; then explaining what he saw. How will his parents react? Will they believe him?

What if his parents go out and Andy stays at home? What if he is watching TV or reading, when he hears a movement upstairs? What if he goes to investigate...?

You decide on the storyline you want. But remember that you must build tension by
▶ keeping the reader guessing
▶ giving details of what Andy sees, hears, smells and feels.
Help the reader to visualize the scene, so that we feel more involved in the action.

2 Imagine you are a detective investigating the events described in *The Trap*. Write your report saying what you think really happened.

Your report might be a collection of different viewpoints, each one paragraph long, like this:

Paragraph 1: Your first impressions when you reach the scene: splintered door, huge trap, man caught in it (nothing too bloodthirsty here – it's a brief factual report).

Paragraph 2: Neighbour 1: account of sounds in the night and seeing the man inspecting his wallflowers next morning.

Paragraph 3: Neighbour 2: noticing the sounds of hammering, etc, as a trap is built. The unusual behaviour of the man.

Paragraph 4: The man's mother or father: what kind of man he was – calm, odd, obsessive?

Paragraph 5: Your conclusion: what you think really happened.

Write your report in a factual style, focusing on details from the poem, plus opinions of people who might have been there.

You could type the report on headed notepaper ('Walton Constabulary') to make it seem more official.

3 How would the poem *The Trap* work as a short story rather than a poem? How would you build the same sense of mystery? Use the opening one or two stanzas and have a go at writing it as a story.

Decisions to make:
- Your point of view: will you tell the story in the first person ('I...') or third person ('He...')?
- Will you give the reader more background about where the action takes place – for example, details about the man's house and garden, and description of the man himself?
- Will you give names to the man and the town or village where he lives, or is it more mysterious if the reader does not know these details?

Poetry
Telling a tale

Aims

In this unit you will:

- ▶ study a poem by a National Curriculum listed pre-1914 poet
- ▶ learn about pronouns and focus on the narrative viewpoint of the poem
- ▶ learn about different forms of rhyme
- ▶ look at a story extract on the same theme as the poem
- ▶ write a poem of your own, or a factual account.

Language focus

First person/third person

All stories have a narrator. This is the name for the person telling the story.

If the narrator was involved in the action, and is telling a story in which they took part, this is called first person narrative. The narrator uses the pronouns 'I', 'me', and 'myself'.

e.g. <u>I</u> woke up this morning. <u>I</u> was late for school, it was pouring with rain and <u>my</u> head was pounding.

If the narrator wasn't involved in the action and didn't take part in the story, 'I' won't appear. Instead, the narrator will refer to the characters by name or will use the pronouns 'he', 'she', 'they'. This is called third person narrative.

e.g. <u>Matthew</u> woke up. <u>He</u> was late for school, it was pouring with rain and <u>his</u> head was pounding.

Pronouns

Pronouns are words which replace nouns, e.g.:

<u>The sea</u> is blue and calm.
<u>It</u> is blue and calm.

<u>Sam and John</u> were going fishing.
<u>They</u> were going fishing.

The pronouns you need to know are:

	Singular	Plural
1st person pronouns	I	we
2nd person pronouns	you	you
3rd person pronouns	he, she, it	they

Rhyme

Rhyme is often used in poetry to create patterns of similar sounds.

Words are said to rhyme when their end sounds match, or sound the same. There are many different types of rhyme:

End rhyme When the last word in a line of poetry is the rhyming word.

Internal rhyme When a word in the middle of a line rhymes with the word at the end of the line.

Full rhyme When two words rhyme completely e.g. 'cry', 'dry' and 'sigh'; 'heaven' and 'Devon'.

Sight rhyme Where two words look from their spelling as if they should rhyme, but in fact the sounds of the words do not rhyme e.g. 'love' and 'move'; 'cost' and 'post'.

Rhyming couplet A rhyme scheme where one line of poetry rhymes with the very next line that comes after it.

TEXT A

William Blake was born in London in 1757. He lived there all his life, and many of his poems show the harshness of life in eighteenth-century London. Blake was largely self-taught, and at the age of fourteen he was apprenticed to an engraver. Blake printed his poems himself, illustrated by his own engravings. His most popular poems are the *Songs of Innocence* published in 1789. The poem in this unit, *The Chimney Sweeper*, is from that collection and shows Blake's horror at the terrible conditions in which many children were forced to live. In the late eighteenth and early nineteenth centuries, the only heating was by open fires.

The chimneys in houses had to be cleaned regularly, and this was often done by having small boys climb up the chimneys to sweep them.

The Chimney Sweeper

When my mother died I was very young,
And my father sold me while yet my tongue
Could scarcely cry ''weep! 'weep! 'weep! 'weep!'
So your chimneys I sweep, & in soot I sleep.

There's little Tom Dacre, who cried when his head,
That curl'd like a lamb's back, was shav'd: so I said
'Hush, Tom! never mind it, for when your head's bare
You know that the soot cannot spoil your white hair.'

And so he was quiet, & that very night,
As Tom was a-sleeping, he had such a sight!
That thousands of sweepers, Dick, Joe, Ned & Jack,
Were all of them lock'd up in coffins of black.

And by came an Angel who had a bright key,
And he open'd the coffins & set them all free;
Then down a green plain leaping, laughing, they run,
And wash in a river, and shine in the Sun.

Then naked & white, all their bags left behind,
They rise upon clouds and sport in the wind;
And the Angel told Tom, if he'd be a good boy,
He'd have God for his father, & never want joy.

And so Tom awoke; and we rose in the dark,
And got with our bags & our brushes to work.
Tho' the morning was cold, Tom was happy & warm;
So if all do their duty they need not fear harm.

William Blake

WORD BANK

sport play, lark about
'weep! 'weep! 'weep! 'weep!
  (a) the usual meaning of weep, meaning to cry; (b) the way the boys advertised their trade by shouting, 'Sweep! sweep!' through the streets. The very young children, in the poem, cannot yet pronounce the 'sw' sound, so the word comes out as 'weep'.

Language questions

1 Make a list of all the pronouns in stanza 1.

2 Rewrite the following lines from the poem, replacing the underlined nouns with pronouns:
a) As <u>Tom</u> was a-sleeping he had such a sight!
b) That thousands of <u>sweepers</u>, Dick, Joe, Ned, & Jack
   Were all of them lock'd up in coffins of black.
c) Tho' the morning was cold, <u>Tom</u> was happy and warm.

3 Do you think the poem is written as a first person or a third person narrative?
   Answer in a full sentence.
Hint Look in particular at the pronouns in the first and last stanzas.

4 Look carefully at the way rhyme is used in *The Chimney Sweeper*. Look back at the different kinds of rhyme listed earlier in this unit (page 126). Then see if you can find one example of each from the poem. Write them under these headings:

▸ End rhyme
▸ Internal rhyme
▸ Full rhyme
▸ Sight rhyme
▸ Rhyming couplet

Comprehension

Answer the questions below in full sentences:

1 What has happened to the narrator's mother?

2 How did the narrator become a chimney sweeper?

3 a) Why did the other boy, Tom Dacre, cry?
   b) How did the narrator try to comfort him?

4 The middle three stanzas of the poem tell the reader about Tom's dream. What does Tom dream of?

5 What are the effects of the dream on Tom the next morning? Include in your answer a short phrase from the poem that tells us how Tom feels.

6 What do you think the narrator's attitude is to his life as a chimney-sweep? Is he angry, accepting, depressed, bitter? Write your answer in full sentences and look carefully for clues in the poem which you can use in your answer.

7 Many things in the poem are either white or black, light or dark. Complete the spider diagrams below by looking carefully through the poem for examples.

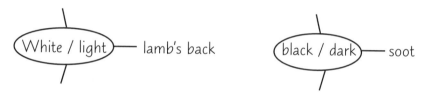

White / light —— lamb's back   black / dark —— soot

8 What do you think these two opposites represent in the poem?
Hint There are two 'worlds' in the poem: the real life of the boys climbing chimneys and the unreal world of Tom's dream.

9 Look again at the last line of the poem. Do you think this is the message Blake intends us to take from the poem? Is it true that if the boys are good and 'do their duty' then they 'need not fear harm'? What do you think Blake wants us to feel after reading this poem? Write a paragraph on what you think the message of the poem is.

TEXT B

The following text is the opening of a children's fantasy story written by Charles Kingsley in 1863. The novel tells the story of Tom, a young chimney-sweep...

The Water Babies

Once upon a time there was a little chimney-sweep, and his name was Tom. That is a short name, and you have heard it before, so you will not have much trouble in remembering it. He lived in a great town in the North country, where there were plenty of chimneys to sweep, and plenty of money for Tom to earn and his master to spend. He could not read nor write, and did not care to do either; and he never washed himself, for there was no water up the court where he lived. He had never been taught to say his prayers. He never had heard of God, or of Christ, except in words which you never have heard, and which it would have been well if he had never heard. He cried half his time, and laughed the other half. He cried when he had to climb the dark flues, rubbing his poor knees and elbows raw; and when the soot got into his eyes, which it did every day in the week; and when his master beat him, which he did every day in the week; and when he had not enough to eat, which happened every day in the week likewise. And he laughed the other half of the day, when he was tossing halfpennies with the other boys, or playing leapfrog over the posts, or bowling stones at the horses' legs as they trotted by, which last was excellent fun, when there was a wall at hand behind which to hide. As for chimney-sweeping, and being hungry, and being beaten, he took all that for the way of the world, like the rain and snow and thunder, and stood manfully with his back to it till it was over, as his old donkey did to a hail-storm; and then shook his ears and was as jolly as ever; and thought of the fine times coming, when he would be a man, and a master sweep, and sit in the public-house with a quart of beer and a long pipe, and play cards for silver money, and wear velveteens and ankle-jacks, and keep a white bull-dog with one grey ear, and carry her puppies in his pocket, just like a man. And he would have apprentices, one, two, three, if he could. How he would bully them, and knock them about, just as his master did to him; and make them carry home the soot sacks, while he rode before them on his donkey, with a pipe in his mouth and a flower in his button-hole, like a king at the head of his army. Yes, there were good times coming; and, when his master let him have a pull at the leavings of his beer, Tom was the jolliest boy in the whole town.

Charles Kingsley

> **WORD BANK**
>
> **ankle-jacks** boots reaching above the ankle
> **flue** a chimney
> **velveteens** trousers made of velvet fabric

Comparison

1 Complete the chart below, showing what you learn from the two texts about the lives of young chimney-sweeps. In the first column list all the facts you can find; then tick in columns two and/or three to show in which texts you found this information. See if you can find six more facts.

Information about sweeps	The Chimney Sweeper	The Water Babies
They were not taught to read or write		✓
The boys slept in soot and were rarely washed	✓	✓

Using your chart from question 1, say which text gives you more factual information about the boys' lives. Write your answer in full sentences. Use details from the text to back up your answer.

The first text, *The Chimney Sweeper*, is a first person narrative: it is written from the point of view of a young chimney-sweep, using 'I' and 'me'. The second text is written as a third person narrative. What differences do you think this creates?

Hint Think about which boy we sympathize with the most, which boy's feelings we find out most about, and which text makes the boys' experiences more real.

Which text do you think is the most effective at making us feel sympathy for the boys? Try to give at least three reasons in your answer. Use details from the texts to support your ideas.

Hint Think about who is the narrator of each text, the way the writers use specific details and language to portray the boys' lives, and the way the texts imagine the boys' futures.

Write a short paragraph explaining which text you preferred. Your answers to questions 2, 3 and 4 should help you. You could include your views on:

▸ which text tells you more about the conditions in which the boy chimney-sweeps lived
▸ how the boys feel about their lives
▸ the writers' use of language
▸ the different narrative viewpoints
▸ your personal responses to the texts.

Speaking and listening

Pairs
Work with a partner. One of you will act as interviewer. The other will play a nineteenth-century boy chimney-sweep. The

interviewer must find out as much as he or she can about conditions at the time.

If you are playing the chimney-sweep, look back at the notes you made for Comprehension question 1.

If you are playing the interviewer, jot down some questions you would like to ask the sweep – about

▶ how they came to be a sweep

▶ what the work is like

▶ how they are treated

▶ what their ambitions and hopes for the future are.

When you are ready, start your role play.

 ②   Class

Should children be allowed to work at all?

Children are no longer sent up chimneys – but many young people choose to work in their spare time, to earn extra money and sometimes to help out in the family's business. Should this be allowed?

Start by dividing into two groups.

One group is going to argue **in favour** of allowing children to work.

The other group is going to argue **against** it.

Make notes on the arguments you will use. Here are a few ideas to get you started:

For	Against
It doesn't do young people any harm.	Adults <u>have</u> to work hard — children should spend time playing, having interests of their own and seeing friends, while they can.
It's easier to get a job when you leave school if you already have some experience.	Some jobs could be dangerous.

Writing assignments

1 Think of a job or occupation which has an element of difficulty or hardship about it. For example: a teacher, a football manager, a park keeper, a milkman, a bus driver. When you have chosen one, you need to brainstorm everything you can think of which you associate with that job.

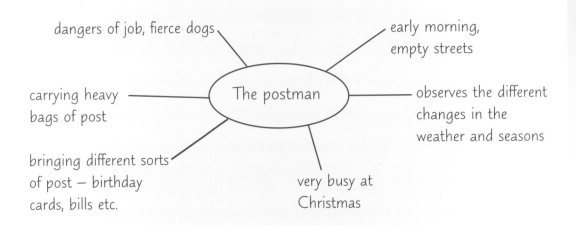

dangers of job, fierce dogs

early morning, empty streets

carrying heavy bags of post

The postman

observes the different changes in the weather and seasons

bringing different sorts of post – birthday cards, bills etc.

very busy at Christmas

Now you are going to use these ideas to write a poem from the point of view of this person. Use the person's job as your poem's title, just as William Blake calls his poem: *The Chimney Sweeper*. Remember you are writing as if you are the person in the poem, using the pronouns 'I' and 'me'.

Arrange your ideas into different stanzas so that your poem shows us what working life is like for this person and how he or she feels about their job. You may wish to borrow Blake's idea of having the person's dream included in the poem, e.g. a postman might dream of delivering a lottery winner's cheque and being given a huge gift in thanks!

2 From what you have learnt from studying the two texts in this unit, write a first person account of a day in the life of a child chimney-sweep from the nineteenth century. Remember these children were often very young, had no living parents and had received little or no education. It is unlikely they could read or write, so try to make your account seem as if the child were speaking rather than writing about his life.

If you did Speaking and Listening activity 1, you might like to look back at the notes you made to help you with this writing assignment.

3 Write an entry for a historical encyclopedia, on child chimney-sweeps. The encyclopedia is aimed at 8–11 year olds. Your entry should be only fifty words long. See how many important facts you can include – you may have to decide to leave some out.

List your facts first.

Then write your entry. Try to keep your style clear and formal, so it is easy to read. Remember that you are writing for younger readers, so your vocabulary needs to be simple and your sentences should be clear and not too long.

Poetry
Finding a voice

Aims

In this unit you will:
- study a poem by a poet from another culture or tradition
- learn about dialect and accent
- focus on features of Black English dialect
- prepare a group reading of a poem
- put forward your own views about poetry.

Language focus

There are many variations of English spoken in the world today. There are differences in the actual words spoken, the way words are pronounced and the way words are put together to form sentences.

It is easy to confuse the terms 'accent' and 'dialect'. However, they are very different things.

Accent

This refers only to the way speakers pronounce words, the way they sound.

Dialect

A dialect is a variation of a language which has its own grammar rules and its own words and expressions. All English dialects share in common most features of the English language; this is why they are classed as dialects and not separate languages.

Standard English

In the past two hundred years one particular dialect of English, known as 'Standard English', has been accepted as being the most formal and 'correct' variety of English. This is the English you will read in textbooks and hear spoken by newscasters on television. Standard English is a dialect and so can be spoken by speakers with many different regional accents: Standard English spoken by someone from Yorkshire will sound different to Standard English spoken by someone from Cornwall.

However, the vocabulary and grammar rules of Standard English remain always the same and do not vary from region to region.

Examples of dialect forms	Standard English
I didn't like <u>none</u> of them.	I didn't like <u>any</u> of them.
Look at <u>them</u> boys over there.	Look at <u>those</u> boys over there.
We <u>was</u> about to go home.	We <u>were</u> about to go home.
It <u>ain't</u> really raining much.	It <u>isn't</u> really raining much.
He ran away really <u>quick</u>.	He ran away really <u>quickly</u>.

Black English

Black English is a dialect form of English that has developed because of particular historical circumstances. In the eighteenth and early nineteenth centuries, many Black Africans were forcibly taken from their homelands and sold into slavery. The slaves often spoke different languages and so they developed new forms of language called 'creoles' so they could communicate with each other and with the white landowners. In the twentieth century there has been a lot of emigration of black people to Britain, USA and Canada and so the growth of different Black English dialects in these countries has continued.

TEXT A

Benjamin Zephaniah was born in Birmingham in 1958. He was brought up in Jamaica and Handsworth. He himself says he was described as a 'born failure' at school and left with no qualifications. He finally turned to music and poetry after serving a short prison sentence. He is now one of Britain's best-known rap and performance poets. He has written a number of poetry collections for both children and adults and travels widely performing his own work in schools, prisons, youth clubs and theatres.

Dis Poetry

Dis poetry is like a riddim dat drops
De tongue fires a riddim dat shoots like shots
Dis poetry is designed fe rantin
Dance hall style, Big mouth chanting,
Dis poetry nar put yu to sleep
Preaching follow me
Like yu is blind sheep,
Dis poetry is not Party Political
Not designed fe dose who are critical.

Dis poetry is wid me when I gu to me bed
It gets into me Dreadlocks
It lingers around me head
Dis poetry goes wid me as I pedal me bike
I've tried Shakespeare, Respect due dere
But dis is de stuff I like.

Dis poetry is not afraid of going ina book
Still dis poetry need ears fe hear an eyes fe hav a look
Dis poetry is Verbal Riddim, no big words involved
An if I hav a problem de riddim gets it solved,
I've tried to be more Romantic, it does nu good for me
So I tek a Reggae Riddim an build me poetry,
I could try be more personal
But you've heard it all before,
Pages of written words not needed
Brain has many words in store,
Yu could call dis poetry Dub Ranting
De tongue plays a beat
De body starts skanking,

Dis poetry is quick an childish
Dis poetry is fe de wise an foolish,
Anybody can do it fe free,
Dis poetry is fe yu an me,
Don't stretch yu imagination
Dis poetry is fe de good of de Nation,
Chant,
In de morning
I chant
In de night
I chant
In de darkness
An under de spotlight,
I pass thru University
I pass thru Sociology
An den I got a Dread degree
In Dreadfull Ghettology.

Dis poetry stays wid me when I run or walk
An when I am talking to meself in poetry I talk,
Dis poetry is wid me,
Below me an above,
Dis poetry's from inside me
It goes to yu
WID LUV.

Benjamin Zephaniah

WORD BANK

dreadlocks Rastafarian hairstyle where hair is twisted into tight ringlets

reggae West Indian/Caribbean style of music

dub rhythmic, improvised verses

skanking a swinging or jerking style of dancing to reggae music

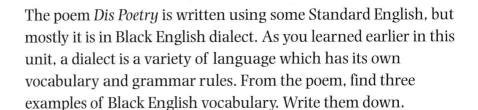

Language questions

1 The poem *Dis Poetry* is written using some Standard English, but mostly it is in Black English dialect. As you learned earlier in this unit, a dialect is a variety of language which has its own vocabulary and grammar rules. From the poem, find three examples of Black English vocabulary. Write them down.

2 Study the following quotations from the poem. For each one:

▶ write a Standard English version
▶ try to explain how the grammar rules of Black English differ from those of Standard English in the examples.

An answer to the first question is given as an example. (The Black English grammatical forms are underlined in the quotations.)

a) 'Like <u>yu is</u> blind sheep'

> Standard English: 'Like you are blind sheep'
> With the pronoun 'you', Black English uses the 'is' form of the verb 'be'; while Standard English uses 'you are'.

b) 'Dis poetry goes wid me as I pedal <u>me</u> bike'
c) 'dis poetry need ears <u>fe hear</u> an eyes <u>fe hav</u> a look'
d) 'I could <u>try be</u> more personal'
e) 'Don't stretch <u>yu</u> imagination'

3 The other noticeable feature of Black English is the non-Standard English spelling of many words. The spelling in Black English is **phonetic**. This means words are spelt using letters that match exactly the sound of the words. In *Dis Poetry*, the poet uses phonetic spelling to represent the Black English accent. (Remember accent refers to the way a speaker pronounces words and is separate to dialect.)
Copy out and complete the chart below showing Black English and Standard English spellings of words. Sometimes you will have to fill in the Black English spelling and sometimes the Standard English one.

Black English Spelling	Standard English Spelling
riddim	
	that
wid	
	those
gu	
fe	
den	
	love
thru	

4 When you have completed your chart, see if you can find any general rules to describe phonetic spelling in Black English. Which letters in Standard English spelling are replaced with which other letters? Try to explain your findings clearly in a short paragraph.

Comprehension

Answer the following questions in full sentences:

1 Look at the line, 'De tongue fires a riddim dat shoots like shots'.
a) What is the tongue compared to in this line?
b) What does this tell us about the type of poetry the poet writes?

2 From stanza 1, find two things that the poet says his poetry isn't.

3 Who does the poet say 'dis poetry' is for? Find two short quotations from the poem to include in your answer.

4
a) What, according to stanza 3, is the most important ingredient of 'dis poetry'?
b) Now that you have read the whole poem, do you agree that this is its most important feature? Explain what you think in full sentences.

5
In stanza 3, it says, that although this poem is printed in a book, 'dis poetry need ears fe hear an eyes fe hav a look'. What do you think the poet means by this? What does he think is the best way to experience this poem?

6
What is the effect of the repetition of 'I chant/In de' towards the end of stanza 3?

Hint Say the words out loud and listen to the effect of these lines.

7
Why do you think Benjamin Zephaniah has chosen to use capital letters for the last line of the poem? What effect does this have?

8
The whole poem is about how it is different from other kinds of poetry. The poet lists all the special qualities of 'dis poetry'. Write a short paragraph showing:

▶ how you think it differs from other, more traditional poems
▶ what the effect of the rhythm is
▶ what the effect of the rhyme is
▶ what the effect of writing a poem in Black English dialect is
▶ what you liked most about the poem.

Speaking and listening

1 **Pairs**

Look at these two opposing views about *Dis Poetry*.

> I think this is a really brilliant poem. It's fresh and young and actually uses the sort of language people use in real life. If poems like this were read in schools, kids would be more keen on poetry.

> *I think it's ridiculous to read poems like this at school – no wonder children today can't spell or speak proper English! A poem like this is full of slang, misspelt words and bad grammar. Poems should set a better example to pupils!*

a) Working in pairs, take each speaker's views in turn. Discuss what other arguments they each might use to support their view.

b) In groups, or even as a whole class debate, discuss your own views on this subject. Which speaker do you most agree with and why?

2 **Group**

Prepare a group reading of the poem which highlights the poem's strong use of rhythm and rhyme. You may like to rap the poem or set it to music. Be adventurous!

TEXT B

Here is another poem in which the writer discusses what poetry should be like and what it means to him.

John Hegley was born in London but spent most of his childhood in Luton. After university in Bradford, he had many jobs, including working in a children's theatre and as a bus conductor. He has published many collections of poetry including *Glad to Wear Glasses*, *Five Sugars, Please*, and *Love Cuts*. His poems appeal to readers of all ages who appreciate a quirky look at life.

Poetry

poetry don't have to be
living in a library
there's poetry that you can see
in the life of everybody,
a lick of paint's the kind of thing I mean
a lick of paint's a lovely piece of writing
the tongue of the paintbrush
giving something drab
a dab new sheen
a lick of paint's exciting.

there are folk who like to see
Latin in their poetry
and plenty of obscurity
me for instance
(only joking)
how I like to listen to the lingo
in bingo
legs eleven
clickety-click
a lick of paint
no – sorry that ain't one

poetry – language on a spree
I want to be
a leaf on the poetree
poetry is good for me
I think I'll have some for my tea

John Hegley

WORD BANK

legs eleven bingo callers' slang for the number eleven
lingo vocabulary of a special subject or group of people
obscurity things which are unclear or not easily understood

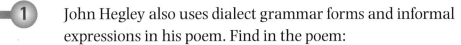

Comparison

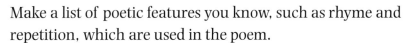

1 John Hegley also uses dialect grammar forms and informal expressions in his poem. Find in the poem:
a) an example of a non-Standard English sentence structure
b) an example of informal vocabulary.

2 Make a list of poetic features you know, such as rhyme and repetition, which are used in the poem.

For each poetic feature you list, include a short quotation from the poem as an example.

3 Both poets agree that poems need not be dull and traditional to be defined as poetry. What does Text B say poetry doesn't have to be or have?

4 Write one or two paragraphs comparing the two poems, showing how they are both about the same subject.
Remember: to compare means to find similarities <u>and</u> differences.

You may like to use the following questions as a guide of what to include in your comparison.

- Are the poems written in the first person or in the third person? (Do they use 'I' or 'he'?)
- Do the narrators' personalities come through in the poems? How?
- Do the two texts agree or disagree about what is meant by 'poetry'?
- How do the poems use poetic features like rhyme, repetition and rhythm?
- Do the poems themselves fit their poets' definitions of what is a good poem?
- Which poem do you feel is the most effective and why?

Writing assignments

1 In his poem, John Hegley says he wants to be 'a leaf on the poetree'.

Write a shape poem called 'The Poetree', either individually or as a group, about how words are used in poetry.

Your poem should be in the shape of a tree – the poetree. You can use a tree outline or, if writing a group poem, have different 'branches' written by different group members.

The poem could include clusters of your favourite words, features of poetry you particularly like: e.g. word or sound patterns, different sorts of rhyme; and quotations from poems you have enjoyed reading.

Your poem does not have to tell a story, it can just celebrate the power of words, the way they sound and the way they make patterns together.

2 Imagine that at school a debating competition is announced which has as its theme 'What we should learn at school'. Write the text of your speech for the competition in which you either argue for or against the studying of poetry at school. You can use quotations or examples from the two texts in this unit as part of your speech, if you want to.

Glossary

Accent   The way somebody pronounces words, which usually depends on where they were brought up or the people they have spent most time with.

Adjective   A word that describes a noun and adds more information to it, e.g. *a **red** balloon*; *a **happy** girl*; *a **fine** day*.

Adverb   A word that describes a verb and adds more information to it, e.g. *she turned **suddenly***; *he spoke **quietly***.

Apostrophe   The punctuation mark (') which can be used in two ways:
1   to show that a letter or group of letters has been missed out, e.g. *I'm not going*; *We'll be there.*
2   to show that someone owns or has something, e.g. *Colin's dad*; *Mary's desk.*

Audience   The people a piece of writing is aimed at; or the people who watch a film, play, or television programme.

Base form (of word)   The main part of a word without prefixes or suffixes, e.g. the base form of *unhappy* is *happy*. Also called the **root** of a word.

Black English   A dialect form of English which is spoken by black people and borrows words and grammar from creoles.

Character   A person in a story, play, or poem.

Characterization   Everything that goes into creating a full and rounded character. This can include the things they think, say and do, how they look, and how they get on with other people.

Clause   A part of a sentence which is actually made up of a simple sentence. Some sentences have a **main clause** and a **subordinate clause**, e.g. *I was washing my hair* (main clause) *when the bell rang* (subordinate clause). The **main clause** can stand on its own and still make sense. The **subordinate clause** adds extra meaning to the sentence but does not make sense on its own.

Colon   A punctuation mark (:) which shows that there is something else to follow in the sentence.

Comparison   A way of describing one thing by saying it is like another, e.g. *The fence was broken into stumps **like a tramp's teeth***.

Complex sentence   A sentence which contains more than one idea and can be made up of several clauses. [See page 7 for information on how complex sentences are made up.]

Creole   A language made up from a combination of a European language and, usually, an African language. [See page 137 for information on how creoles came to exist.]

Dialect   A variation of a language, which has its own grammatical rules and its own words and expressions. A dialect is usually spoken by people who come from a particular area or cultural background.

Dialogue   The words spoken by the characters in a play or story.

Discourse markers   Words and phrases which link a text together and help the reader follow how the text is developing, e.g. *then, later, therefore, whilst*.

Elided words   Words which have been joined together, with some of the letters missed out, e.g. ***we're** going* (not *we are*); ***they'll** be there* (not *they will*).

End rhyme   A rhyme where the last word of a line of poetry rhymes with the last word of another line.

Exclamation mark   The punctuation mark (!) used at the end of a sentence. It can show, for example, that a command has been given or that something is said urgently or in surprise, e.g. *'Come here!'*; *'I can't!'*; *It was Joe!*

Fact   Something that is true, and not just an opinion, e.g. *The Earth moves around the Sun*.

First person   The *I* form of the verb, e.g. *I walked to the door*.

Formal language   Language which does not contain slang, and where all or most of the sentences are complete and 'grammatically correct' (i.e. in Standard English).

Full rhyme   A rhyme where two words rhyme completely, e.g. *cry / dry; full / pull*.

Informal language   Language that breaks the rules of grammar by using slang, changing sentence structure and sometimes appearing more like spoken than written language.

Internal rhyme   A rhyme where a word in the middle of a line rhymes with the one at the end.

Legend   A traditional story, which might contain some truth but which cannot be proved.

Main clause   See **Clause**.

Narrative viewpoint   The character through whose eyes a story is told. In *Jake felt his anger growing*, the viewpoint is Jake's; in *Sara realized Jake was angry*, the viewpoint is Sara's.

Narrator   The person who tells a story. This can be a person who tells the story from the outside, or someone who is involved in the story [see also **Narrative viewpoint**].

Noun   The word in a sentence which labels a person, place, thing, idea, or feeling, e.g. *Jenny felt a **wave** of **tiredness** as she walked down the **street***.

Noun phrase   A group of words built around a noun. The extra words add detail to the noun, e.g. *the bus* could become *the uncomfortable old red bus* in a noun phrase.

Opinion   Something that is not a fact, but someone's point of view, e.g. *The garden is **charming***.

Paragraph   A block of sentences linked by one overall idea or topic, e.g. the paragraph *Helping to Hear* on page 11 contains three sentences, all on the same subject.

Personification   Writing about an object or an idea as if it were a person, e.g. *The computer **is in a bad mood** today*.

Phonetic   To do with the sounds in words. Phonetic spelling is based on how words are pronounced, rather than how they are usually written down.

Phrase   A group of words which makes sense inside a clause or sentence, but cannot stand on its own, e.g. *running around*; *on a bike*.

Prefix   An element that we add to the beginning of a word to change its meaning, e.g. *un-* (not), *re-* (again).

Presentational devices   Ways of laying out a text, also known as 'design features', such as titles, captions, bullet points, and bold lettering. [See page 7 for a list of presentational devices used in non-fiction texts.]

Pronoun   A word that can replace a noun, to avoid repetition, e.g. *I, it, he, she, they, we.*

Pun   A sort of joke made by using a word or phrase that can have more than one meaning, or that sounds very like a phrase with a different meaning, e.g. *Ornamental stones now at **rock bottom** prices: rock* as in 'stones' and *rock bottom* meaning 'cheap'.

Punctuation   The marks we use in writing to make it easier to read and understand. [See also **Apostrophe, Colon, Exclamation mark, Question mark**.]

Purpose   The reason a writer has for writing a text; e.g. to give information, to persuade somebody, or to entertain.

Question mark   The punctuation mark (?) used at the end of a sentence to show it is a question, e.g. *Who are you?*

Rhyme   Words rhyme when their endings have the same sounds, e.g. *bend / send.*

Rhyme scheme   The pattern of rhymes inside a poem.

Rhyming couplet   A rhyme scheme where one line of poetry rhymes with the line that comes next after it, e.g.
Mary had a little lamb
She tried to feed it peas and ham.

Rhythm   The 'beat' of a poem. The rhythm might be fast, smooth, or irregular, for example. A limerick has a very noticeable rhythm.

Root   See **Base form**.

Sight rhyme   A rhyme where two words look as if they should rhyme, although they don't when you read them out loud, e.g. *although / through; cow / mow.*

Simple sentence   A sentence which is made of only one clause and which has only one main point, e.g. *Alan joined* *the football team*. The meaning of a simple sentence is very clear.

Slang   A very informal kind of language, often belonging to a particular group of people, e.g. army slang, Australian slang.

Stage directions   The instructions telling an actor how to speak or move on the stage, and what emotions to show.

Standard English   A dialect of English which is accepted as the most formal and 'correct' form of English. It is the English used by newsreaders and in textbooks.

Stanza   A group of lines in a poem (also called a verse). Each stanza is separated from the next by a space.

Subordinate clause   See **Clause**.

Tabloid newspaper   A newspaper with a small format, aimed at general readers. Tabloid newspapers have large headlines and lots of pictures. They often focus on stories about famous people, crime, and scandals.

Third person   The form of the verb which uses *he*, *she*, or *they*, e.g. *Laura walked to the door*; *William remembered where he had left the keys*.

Tone   The atmosphere of a piece of writing: whether it is serious or comic, for example.

Verb   The word in a sentence which says what people or things are doing, e.g. *He **danced** and **sang***; or what they are being, e.g. *The room **was** dark*.

Acknowledgements

We are grateful for permission to reprint the following copyright material.

ABCNEWS report by Gina Smith: 'Bionic Man is on the Horizon', June 23 1998, Copyright © 1998 ABCNEWS and Starwave Corporation; Rachel Anderson: extract from 'Black and White', copyright © Rachel Anderson 1995, from Michael Morpurgo (ed): *Muck and Magic* (Heinemann and Mammoth 1995), reprinted by permission of the author; Richard Curtis: extract from script of *The Vicar of Dibley*, Episode One: 'The Arrival', © Vicar of Dibley: a BBC production written by Richard Curtis, reprinted by permission of The Peters Fraser & Dunlop Group Ltd on behalf of Richard Curtis; Dorling Kindersley extract from *Eyewitness Guide, Future* (1998), reprinted by permission of Dorling Kindersley; Gerald Durrell: extract from *The Baffut Beagles* (Grafton, Wm Collins, 1954), copyright Gerald Durrell, reprinted by permission of Curtis Brown Ltd, London, on behalf of the Estate of Gerald Durrell; Mike Harding: extract from *Walking the Dales* (Michael Joseph, 1986), reprinted by permission of Penguin Books Ltd.; Seamus Heaney: 'Mid-term Break' from *Death of a Naturalist* (1966), reprinted by permission of the publisher, Faber & Faber Ltd.; John Hegley: 'Poetry' from *Can I Come Down Now, Dad?* (Methuen, 1991), reprinted by permission of Methuen Publishing Ltd.; Mary Morris: extract from *Two Weeks with the Queen* (Macmillan Children's Books, 1994) adapted from the novel by Morris Gleitzman; Nidderdale Chamber of Trade, information from website, http://www.nidderdale.co.uk, reprinted by permission of the Secretary, George Sewell, Telephone 01765 608277; Philippa Pearce: extract from 'The Dog Got Them' from *The Shadow Cage and Other Stories of the Supernatural* (Viking Kestrel, 1977), reprinted by permission of Penguin Books Ltd.; Gervase Phinn: extract from *The Other Side of the Dale* (Michael Joseph, 1998), copyright © Gervase Phinn 1998, reprinted by permission of Penguin Books Ltd.; Tony Robinson and Richard Curtis: extract from *Theseus, Monster Killer* (first published 1988 BBC/Knight), reprinted by permission of Hodder & Stoughton Ltd.; George Bernard Shaw: extract from *St Joan* (Penguin, 1946), reprinted by permission of The Society of Authors, on behalf of the Bernard Shaw Estate; Jon Stallworthy: 'The Trap' from *The Apple Barrel* (1974), copyright © Oxford University Press 1961, 1963, reprinted by permission of the publisher, Oxford University Press; The Sun article 'Royal Hatscot' by Paul Thompson from The Sun, London, 16 June 1999, copyright © News International Newspapers Limited, 1999, reprinted by permission of News International Newspapers Ltd.; Vauxhall Motors extract from Vauxhall Corsa SXi special edition leaflet, August 1998, reprinted by permission of Vauxhall Motors Ltd.; Benjamin Zephaniah: 'Dis Poetry' from *City Psalms* (Bloodaxe Books, 1992), reprinted by permission of the publisher.

Although every effort has been made to trace and contact copyright holders before publication this has not been possible in some cases. If notified the publisher will be pleased to rectify any errors or omissions at the earliest opportunity.

We would like to thank the following for permission to include photographs:

p8 Science Photo Library, Ronald Grant Archive, Evening Standard, Science and Society Picture Library (The Bionic Human Being), Chas. A. Blatchford & Sons Ltd (boy on bike), Rex Features Ltd (Revolutionary leg), all reproduced by kind permission of Dorling Kindersley; p16/17 Science Photo Library Ltd; p22 Vauxhall Motors Ltd; p28 Times Newspapers Ltd (bottom left), John Stillwell/PA (top left, top right, bottom centre); p32 Gervase Phinn; p33 The Bridgeman Art Library Ltd/Simon Marsden; p38 John Morrison; p39 J Allan Cash Ltd; p44 The Bridgeman Art Library Ltd; p45 AKG London; p47 Corbis UK Ltd; p50 Photostage/Donald Cooper; p56 Peters Fraser & Dunlop; p57/60/61 BBC; p69 Puffin Books/Martin Salter; p70 Alan Brodie Representation; p71 Photostage/Donald Cooper; p81 Camera Press Ltd/Martin Godwin; p82 Corbis UK Ltd; p87 Camera Press Ltd; p89 Corbis UK Ltd; p93 Camera Press Ltd; p94 Bruce Coleman Collection; p101 Scope Features; p102 John Morrison; p106 Rex Features Ltd (top); p106 Peters Fraser & Dunlop; p113 Oxford University Press; p119 Carcanet Press; p120 Tony Stone Images; p126/127 Mary Evans Picture Library Ltd; p129 Bridgeman Art Library/C.H. Jeens; p130 AKG Photo London; p137 National Portrait Gallery/Miriam Reik; p138/9 Tony Stone Images; p143 Camera Press Ltd/Kev Dutton; p144 Corbis UK Ltd.

We would like to thank the following for permission to include illustrations:

p107 Chris Smedley reproduced by kind permission of Hodder Headline; p114 Peter Melnyczuk.

Cover image: Image Bank/John W Banagan